SAFETY 1st INVESTING

If you'll do for a few years what most people *won't* do, you'll be able to do for the rest of your life what most people *can't* do.

Wade B. Cook

SAFETY

1st

INVESTING

WADE B. COOK

Lighthouse Publishing Group, Inc.
Seattle, Washington

 Lighthouse Publishing Group, Inc.
Copyright © 1999 Wade B. Cook

Library of Congress Cataloging-in-Publication Data
Cook, Wade.
Safety 1st Investing/Wade B. Cook.
p. cm.
ISBN 1-892008-59-9
1. Investments. 2. Finance, Personal. I. Title. II. Title:
Safety first investing.
HG4521.C625   1999
332.6--dc21   99-20560
                                                        CIP

Book Design by Judy Burkhalter
Dust Jacket by Angela Wilson
Dust Jacket Photo by Vaughn Tanner
Dust Jacket Illustration by Jason Woodruff
Technical Assistance by Bethany McVannel, Amy Jo Gilson,
Mark Engelbrecht, Brent Magarrell,
Cynthia Fliege, and Cheryl Rhodes

Published by Lighthouse Publishing Group, Inc.
14675 Interurban Avenue South
Seattle, WA 98168-4664
1-800-706-8657
206-901-3100 (fax)

Source Code: SFI99

Printed in the United States of America
10 9 8 7 6 5 4 3

To:

Dean Bennion,
   Randy Carlson,
      Peter Stolcer,
         Roger Mankus,
my stockbrokers. Thank you for teaching me
and caring about our shareholders' money.
I appreciate your patience, great attitudes,
and perseverance.

OTHER BOOKS BY LIGHTHOUSE PUBLISHING GROUP, INC.

Wall Street Money Machine, Wade Cook
Stock Market Miracles, Wade Cook
Bear Market Baloney, Wade Cook
On Track Investing, David Hebert
Rolling Stocks, Gregory Witt
Sleeping Like A Baby, John Hudelson
Making A Living In The Stock Market, Bob Eldridge

101 Ways To Buy Real Estate Without Cash, Wade Cook
Cook's Book On Creative Real Estate, Wade Cook
How To Pick Up Foreclosures, Wade Cook
Owner Financing, Wade Cook
Real Estate For Real People, Wade Cook
Real Estate Money Machine, Wade Cook

Blueprints For Success, Volume 1, Various Authors
Brilliant Deductions, Wade Cook
Million Heirs, John Childers, Jr.
The Secret Millionaire Guide To Nevada Corporations
John Childers, Jr.
Wealth 101, Wade Cook

A+, Wade Cook
Business Buy The Bible, Wade Cook
Don't Set Goals, Wade Cook
Wade Cook's Power Quotes, Volume 1, Wade Cook

Living In Color, Renae Knapp

OTHER BOOKS BY WADE B. COOK

Y2K Gold Rush
Gold Leaf Press

CONTENTS

GRATITUDE

It takes a team to write a book like this. I am also sincerely grateful for the help of my many Team Wall Street instructors who have not only taught our students well, but have shared many of their innovative and up-to-date ideas. The members of our research and trading department George Park, David McKinlay, Rich Simmons, and Jay Harris have given extremely valuable help on a timely basis. Thanks also goes to Lighthouse Publishing and our publications department, Judy Burkhalter and Brent Magarrell who have been very helpful in typesetting and editing this book, and Angela Wilson who designed the cover. There have also been many other contributors to this effort, including Mark Engelbrecht, Bethany McVannel, Jeff Allen, and Amy Jo Gilson for their work on the special reports. Also thanks to the Vice Presidents of Wade Cook Financial Corporation, Bruce Couch, Rick Smith, and Carl Sanders. They run the show so I can write. Also, heartfelt appreciation to my assistants Patsy Sanders and Angela Johnson, and to Robin Andersen, Larry Keim, and Shane Norris. And last, but not least, thanks goes to my wife, Laura, for her love and support.

PREFACE

Life is not too complicated for me. Financially, we all need more cash flow. In many of my seminars I ask how many of the attendees own their own businesses. Usually 25% of the hands go up. I ask, "If you, the business owners, do not go into your place of business (your store, your shop, your office), how long will your business last without you?" There are some low-level comments—almost a murmur. Across the board in America it's two and a half weeks. The average business shuts down in two and a half weeks if the owner doesn't show up.

I then ask, "How many of you work for someone else?" Many more hands go up. Not all of the hands mind you, as there are many retirees in the class. Why these retirees show up is another great topic. Why are they at a cash flow seminar? We'll save that for another time. I ask the employed, "If you don't go to work, when does your income stop?" "Right away," I hear. "Now." "Next Friday."

I pose this, "You've all heard of income producing assets. For most of you, you're it. You are your only income producing asset. If your asset does not show up to work, what happens? No income!"

Then I ask, "Can you have income without assets? No. Something, somebody has to produce the income." I go on, "You can't have income without assets, but can you have assets without income?" I pause, "The answer is "yes." Yes, and far too many of you have far too many of those–assets with no income."

It is income that lets you spend more time with the kids. It is income that lets you go back to school, pay the bills, or give more to your church.

Income, real cash income. My seminars, my home and car study courses, and my books have been about helping people build up a group of assets which will spin-off income. Income to live on.

My educational mission is to help people get more unearned income. To show them how they can change their life out of the "go to work and trade my time for money" routine. Is that what you want? And do you want safety, too? How much risk do you want to take? Safety should be very important–to preserve your principal, your asset base. Can you have great cash flow with safety first?

To this question I answer an emphatic "yes." In fact, to my way of thinking they go hand in hand. How can you learn to build cash flow for now and the future without having your asset base grow? This should happen simultaneously. I teach these principles to any-one who will listen and learn.

Strange. That is the only word I can use to describe the past few years. A national best-selling book on every business, money, or financial list available. *Wall Street Money Machine* has definitely stirred the pot. It's been a wonderful run. I've spoken in dozens of states, been on hundreds of radio and TV talk shows and, boy oh boy, has the criticism been intense.

"Dear Wade,
Over the past few months I have read articles in the news-papers and heard commentary from various sources of naysay-ers in regards to your teachings. These attacks on the principles that you teach bother me, as these self-same principles have changed our lives and propelled us down the path of true suc-cess.

Our story is similar to others, but after recent negative press and the urgings of our wonderful sales/service representative, I have decided to take the time and put our story and thanks, in writing to you, your teachers, and staff.

My wife first heard you on a talk show on Philadelphia radio about two years ago. She called and requested the free tape and purchased your book, *Wall Street Money Machine*. We listened to your tape while driving to Atlantic City for a long weekend to celebrate our anniversary. What we heard made sense! It was logical! We anxiously read the book cover-to-cover. We both concluded that you had an approach that was well founded and decided to sign up for the Wall Street Workshop™.

That was in February 1997. We decided to read, listen and watch tapes, access W.I.N.™ and trade a little before going to class. We established a brokerage account and started with about $10,000 to 15,000. We began by writing covered calls. Then we bought calls. When we attended the class in June, the tuition was paid for by the profits. In class we learned other plays and gained some further understanding. We made trades and profits in class, as many others do.

At this time I should point out that prior to being introduced to your company, we had a brokerage account with stock in that we were "hoping" would increase in value. We owned some mutual funds and had IRAs. Ours is a second marriage and two of our children are in college, one out, and one in 8th grade. My wife is a teacher and I was a business owner. Our joint income was fair and covered expenses, but we were not making money. Our initial goal was to add an extra $1,000 a month to the mix, so we would have money to cover what ever may arise and enjoy life a bit more. We then looked to build that to replace my wife's salary in a few years. During our first year of actual trading (April to December) we made our mistakes, but we had 78% successful trades and booked about a 30% profit in addition to covering the cost of education. I would like to point out that the reason our success was limited during this stage is that we did know our exit UP, but did not plan and exit DOWN. Therefore losers were larger than winners.

This year we changed brokers and made a decision to limit losses on all option plays. Things were going well and we were making money. We attended a Wealth Academy and purchased our first Nevada Corporation. The short Bear Market last summer hurt in some ways but actually provided some excellent buying opportunities that have turned profitable. In August we made a few adjustments in trading style and our account began to grow. Suddenly we were talking about trading as a full time business, but we still needed something more.

In October we attended the Next Step Seminar in Las Vegas. At that time the instructor defined charts and added a key to further success. We were excited! A couple of successful trades that week enabled us to buy a time-share in Las Vegas (perfect for corporate meetings). Now equipped with a new level of knowledge and understanding, our trades got bigger and better. In October we equaled my wife's salary. November was just as good and then you mailed me a tape about "PUTS!" I had some previous success selling puts, but usually I sold puts to buy calls on a stock I thought was going up. I began selling puts that were at the money or in the money. I thought this was great! We were making money and I began to plan to stop working and become a full trader.

Then my wife and I attended a clinic one evening in Philadelphia to a Support class. I signed up that evening. By the time it began, I was selling puts and making money. I was using your meter drop principle and the profits were mounting. Then the instructor took me to the next step of understanding! I began to sell out of the money puts after researching stock splits and other stocks primed to move. As a result of the trades I made in December, we will make more in profits than I ever earned in a year working. I am now consulting a couple days a week, but basically, I am retired and S-E-L-L-I-N-G P-U-T-S!

It is still hard to believe, but it is real! We are anxiously looking forward to our many years of retirement ahead. I have given my son and stepdaughter your books and tapes, so they can begin gaining the knowledge that will secure their financial future. I tell others, but most don't see themselves being able, and as you know, first you must truly believe! This past week it made us feel good to be able to make IRA contributions for our children in addition to ourselves, and to tell my mother that we would be able to pay for my father's tombstone, removing a financial burden from her.

We applaud you for offering the education to anyone willing to remove prejudices and take a chance on a new way of looking at an old market. You have opened our eyes to many new things and changed the way we view the world around us. The people we have encountered in your organization from top to bottom have been first class and you can count on us for a reference any time. Last week we purchased our second corporation and plan to expand the business in the years to come and hopefully our children will follow your directions and enjoy an easier and more rewarding life without limits.

Thank you.

Sincerely,
Mark R. Goodman"

"Dear (Sales Rep)

Sorry if I talked your head off today, I do go on and on. Can't help it. Any time I get the chance to sing the praises of Wade Cook and his people, I never seem to know when or where to stop. My very English wife still refers to Wade as "The Dear, Dear Man." And as I told you on the phone, there is hardly a day that goes by that we don't have reason to say, "Thank you, Wade." Strangely, it isn't just the money we've made, although of course that's a large part of it. We had the great and good pleasure of meeting Wade in Irvine, CA. Recently. I told him that the day before, my wife and I made $25,000, in one day. Well, when we got back home, we repeated it by making another large score, this time for $26,000, all in one day. Now, we don't do that every day to be sure. And I think Wade might be pleased to learn that it wasn't all made on the hi-tech stock. However, today beats all we've ever seen. We made $230,079, today. January 12, 1999. We made it on CMGI. A tech stock. In fact, on January 11th, we made $47,855, on January 7th, we made $46,644. We've made $372,725 in just the opening days of this month. That does not mean we have never lost money. Oh. Boy! Have we lost. But we've NEVER lost a dime when we followed the rules as taught at the Wall Street Workshop™. It was only when human nature took over and we got "greedy," that we ever lost anything. It was only when we got careless. Mostly though, we were on the straight and narrow, as the old saying goes. One of our instructors was a very beautiful and BRILLIANT young lady. One of the things that helps to keep our heads on straight is the fear that we'll do something really dumb; and not be a credit to her and to Wade. If I had been lucky enough to have even one teacher half as good as she is, I'd have stayed in school when I was much younger. A year ago today, we were living on 20 plus credit cards and had a second loan out on our home. Today, we're down to 2 or 3 cards and that second loan has been paid off. And we don't owe much on the cards. Up until August 1st, we did not have a computer. Just a fax machine, and we didn't buy that until we made the money to pay off the credit card we used to attend the Workshop. We made enough in four weeks or so to pay off the tuition. We have since paid for another, which we haven't attended yet, but plan to do so very soon. Oh by the way, our house needed newer windows. The cost is $10,000 plus. We made that in one day recently. There are times we'll want to buy something; maybe we don't even need it. Before we do, my wife usually reminds me of what Wade has to say about foolish spending. The word around our house is "What does Wade have to say, or what would he say about this?" I'll tell the world about Wade Cook, and the great people who teach his seminars. One very last thing before I end up writing a book here. Well, two last things ok? Once, a very long time ago, I drove a cab in El Monte, CA. And finally, a personal message for Wade Cook with regard to each and every one of his critics. May ALL OF HIS CRITICS GET A TERRIBLE CRAMP IN THEIR TONGUE! That's a very old Yiddish curse. But his critics deserve no less.

Very Sincerely yours, and again with much thanks for helping to turn our lives around.

Joel and Jennifer Diamond"

I would love to take on any one of those critics if they would just talk about, or criticize one of my formulas, but they don't. They can't kill the message, so they take on the messenger. Well, they've come and gone, and tens of thousands of my students are doing very, very well. They're quitting jobs, adopting babies, and donating vast sums of money to churches and charities. They are walking the walk that they've always wanted to walk.

"Dear Mr. Cook,

I hope that you will be able to find the time to read my letter. The short version is a thank you of immeasurable depth for what you have provided me. The long version is to tell you what your help has really meant to me.

I am a 46-year old married anesthesiologist with two children. I work very hard in a profession that is not well understood nor appreciated. I have mastered my field as CEO of our corporation and Chairman of the department for the second time. Unfortunately, I am burned out and have for some time been looking for a new field to learn. I knew that I wanted to learn all about investing and the stock market but after a fair amount of research I found there were no reputable educational classes being offered.

Then I attended one of your introductory seminars and immediately signed up for the Wall Street Workshop™, even before I consulted with my wife. As an Amway failure I knew that she would be negative. This is especially true since only in the last month or two have we been able to save any money at all after a three-year recuperation from a significantly failed real estate deal. She is not the one to trust or try anything other than a full time working job.

I have just completed the Wall Street Workshop™ and am now a stock market knowledge junkie. Many of the students want to make significant sums of money. All I need is to make just enough to buy my wife a pair of super nice earrings and to pay for all the courses and she'll be happy. I can't wait to save enough to go to the Cook University. I want the knowledge and then the confidence will come. The earnings will always follow.

My goal now is to succeed enough to become a Wade Cook Wall Street instructor. That is my challenge. Just like it is taught at John Hopkins, see one, do one, teach one.

In the Jewish religion the highest level of giving charity to another is to give them a job or the knowledge of how to provide for themselves.

I can't express enough to you the gratitude I have for your providing me the knowledge and support via your classes. I came as a total neophyte and stock market virgin. I regard what you have done for myself and others, for the opportunity that you have provided.

Simple words, but powerful; THANK YOU.

Sincerely yours,
Mark E. Schutz M.S. M.D."

This is holistic investing. No book exists like this. It would be good to learn the formulas in *Wall Street Money Machine, Stock Market Miracles* and *Bull and Bears* (formerly entitled *Bear Market Baloney*). *Safety 1st Investing* is different. It, at one time, ties together the strategies and puts the emphasis right where it should be–on safety first investing for cash flow.

After years of teaching we now have hundreds and in some cases thousands of letters and testimonials from students which show the results of the use of my formulas. From time to time I'll use them in this book. Why? Because they prove the point. Formulas work. Why? Because maybe you as the reader can relate to these people. You might think, "Well, Wade can do it–what about me?" The stories of these "butchers, bakers, and candlestick makers" might be what you need to gain the desire to learn more.

You'll read of people who knew nothing–beginners. You'll read of their fears, their concerns, and their mistakes. As they go they grow. They want to learn more. That desire to learn more, to learn how to apply the formulas better, to correct themselves and improve is the ultimate formula for success.

I'll pull out excerpts from their testimonials to prove a point. We receive similar comments constantly.

- "I've had 97 to 100% success if I followed the formula."
- "But we've never lost a dime when we followed the rules as taught at the Wall Street Workshop™."
- "I would like to point out that the reason our success was limited is that we did not know our exit." They weren't following the formulas.

I hope this proves the point. If you don't use my formulas, at least discover and create your own. I am always in the learning mode and would like to see what you've observed, discovered, or worked out. Let me know at wadecook.com.

We've made an attempt to verify each testimonial that has been made. Thousands of people have written or called us. Obviously, you won't achieve the actual returns they have achieved. That play is over. We use testimonials to prove the simple point: The use of formulas will increase your ability to make money. Formulas can be learned, fine-tuned, and improved. Each example is or was a snapshot in time. They are given for illustration purposes only. You need to work with your own stockbroker to determine suitability, risk, availability, and current prices. We never give advice. That is the arena of your professional advisors. We teach formulas, strategies, methods and systems. You work over each formula, practice on paper, use your stockbroker, and decide for yourself if this formula or that particular trade is right for you.

Good learning and good luck.

Experience is the best teacher.
The problem is it gives the test first,
the lesson later.

Vernon Law

CHAPTER 1

SAFETY

Will Rogers once said, "I'm not so much worried about the return on my money, as the return of my money." Safety in real estate, safety in business, and safety in the stock market has to have as a core objective the preservation of capital. Assets need to increase in value not decrease. And even before we grow our assets, we must figure out how not to lose value. A famous college basketball coach once said, "The way to win games is to not lose." I agree.

One thing we can do now is get our money out of the way of danger. And hopefully get it in the way of progress as a by-product. Here are a few ponderings:

1. Invest in companies with good earnings. Even if the earnings are not paid out as dividends. Stock prices usually follow earnings, or move in advance of earnings reports. If the earnings dip, take caution. If it's real operational losses then watch out. If it's a one time charge off or a non-recurring expense, maybe use the dip in the stock price to buy more.

2. Be cautious of companies that are betting on the future, i.e., new drug companies with no earnings for years to come. Yes, they may take off, but who knows?. If you see drugs approved, or large company interest in small compa-

ny joint ventures or buyouts, then try to get in the way. Make sure the news is real. Base decisions on facts.

3. Be careful of the "tips" you get. As a cab driver my tips were real. As an investor, I've become weary of hundreds of "tips," all with good intentions, but usually bad advice and bad consequences.

4. When in doubt stay with the big guys (the large cap stocks). Do your homework. Buy when there's the highest likelihood a stock will go up. Constantly look for opportunities to buy. See the section on quarterly merry-go-rounds.

5. Learn your sell points or exit points. Keep your money deployed in the best places. This is not market timing, this is buying wholesale, selling retail.

I'll give safety tips on the use of formulas for cash flow later. But first, you won't find a Wade Cook recommended list of stocks to buy or sell. There are plenty of people who do that. Please don't come to my seminars or workshop looking for a "hot stock tip." It's not my style. Why? I don't think a recommendation serves a purpose unless it fits a plan or a formula.

You see, that's what sets me apart from all the others. They're trying to earn a commission so they have the next "stock buy of the week." You know the grass is always greener on the other side. And they always have a stock or mutual fund to sell.

I'm into building cash flow. You'll read more about this in a different chapter on income generation called Cash Flow, Cash Flow, Cash Flow. I won't bring up the details here, but a quick understanding of its concept is important. This style is new to so many people.

I teach formulas. I hope you buy into this new way of looking at the stock market. A formula is based on logic, observation, correct information, patterns, and an ability to make quick decisions. A formula can be tested–even on paper before using real money. You can measure results. You can expect certain returns. You don't plant carrots and get beans.

Formulas also have a certain time (or situation) when they are used. They are specific, detailed, and definitely learnable. The more precise you are, the better your profits. Learning formulas might be a challenge but the results are phenomenal. I'm going to put a few "extraordinary" testimonials here and then ask a few questions. Please read and ponder each one:

"Dear Wade,

How can I describe my experience at my first Wall Street Workshop™? A deer in the headlights of an oncoming freight train. A child seeing a fire truck screaming by for the first time? An ancient mariner, spying the hazy shape of a strange and distant land? I think it was a combination of all three! I had absolutely no preparation for what I was hearing, I had read none of Wade's books, nor have I had any prior stock market experience. During the class, I understood very little but wrote down everything. "Why didn't somebody tell me about this earlier?" I asked myself repeatedly. At the end of the course, I understood enough to feel like Kyle MacLach in Frank Herbert's Dune, "Father! The sleeper has awakened!"

I embarked on a new mission. I followed all of Wade Cook's instruction. I started a Nevada Corporation. I opened up a corporate brokerage account. I took the "Wall Street Workshop™" three times and The Next Step twice. I also went to The One Minute Commute, SOAR, The Secret Millionaire, Options Bootcamp, The Real Estate Bootcamp and Spread and Butter. And all through this process, I did papertrade after papertrade after papertrade. Did I mention the fact that I did paper trades?

When I couldn't stand watching all this possible money making any longer, I decided the time was right to jump in and get my feet wet. I started with $5,000. I purchased two stocks when I thought they were both poised to take off. They did and when they started to downturn, I wrote covered calls on both stocks. About a week and a half later, the third Thursday came and went and I regained control of my stock. To my good fortune the stocks began to rise again. I wrote a covered call on one and the other one spiked up so fast that when it downturned I sold the stock: In just under 30 days my brokerage account had gone from $5,000 to a whopping $11,600! Now I realize that this kind of return is somewhat of an anomaly, but the gains have not stopped. As of writing this it has been two and a half months since I bought my first stock and my brokerage account is at $15,000. I have tripled my money! I am now employing a "Boxed Covered Call" strategy on Microsoft LEAPS®.

The best part about this is that I am not an accountant or some kind of financial genius. I am a fine artist. I paint large contemporary oils. And this knowledge that Wade has given me is freedom. Freedom to have the time I need to perfect my craft. As far as I'm concerned, every artist in America today should take this course!

Thank you Wade Cook and all of your excellent instructors and staff!

> Sincerely,
> Robert Harris"

"Dear Wade:

Monica and Albert Diedrich came to the U.S. from Argentina more than 20 years ago looking for a better future. They both worked hard to make a living and raise their two boys. For 19 years, Monica owned and operated a successful video rental and repair business, while her husband worked as a supervisor at a large oil company.

Three months ago, Monica decided it was time to sell her lucrative business venture. "I had been working ten hour days for years and wanted something less time consuming," says Monica.

Meanwhile, Albert began hearing about Wade Cook financial investment strategies. "I'd seen several commercials and then saw their program on Channel 22 in Los Angeles. After that, I finally decided to go," says Albert.

He and his wife attended a three hour Wade Cook Financial Clinic where they learned several stock market investment strategies. Albert immediately wanted to continue their training with the company's Wall Street Workshop™, but Monica was reluctant.

"Albert tried to convince me to go for two months," says Monica. "I had been to so many different kinds of seminars in my life that I was fed up with them. I really wasn't interested in the idea of learning something 'new and exciting' about something old. And there were so many people at the Financial Clinic saying so many wonderful things about the workshop that I just couldn't believe it was true."

Finally, Monica gave in. "I didn't want him to do it alone. We both agreed that we would get more out of it if we did it as a team."

Both Monica and Albert attended the workshop in Orange County in June. "After the workshop, we both decided that this could be a viable vehicle to make money," says Monica. "We also knew that we had to approach it as a business–that it would require the same discipline and diligence."

The couple began using the strategies they learned at the workshop. At the end of June, they held their first official "business meeting" to review their finances and see how well they had done. "After adding up the figures, we realized that we had made $5,375 in less than four weeks. I was ecstatic," say Monica.

These days, Monica can be found at the Wade Cook Financial Education Center in Santa Ana, where she continues to apply her workshop strategies. With its bookstore and online stock market information and resources, the center is an ideal location for workshop alumni to meet and interact. "It's not just a place you go to for ticker symbols and stock prices," says Monica. "Talking with other seminar attendees helps you put what you've learned in perspective. It's a very supportive group and I'm always learning new things."

In the several days since Monica and Albert's first business meeting, the couple's cash flow has again increased, this time by an additional $7,500. "It used to be that I was the one opening the blinds in the morning and getting her out of bed," says Albert. "Now she's up at 5:30 AM everyday getting ready to go to the center–just like a job."

Says Monica: "It works. That's the bottom line. If you apply what you're learning and have the patience, you'll get the results. My accountant had warned me over and over again not to get into the stock market. But after attending the Workshop, I knew I could make it work. Now I'm going to give him one of Wade Cook's stock market strategy tapes and insist that he go. You really can succeed in the stock market by using these strategies."

And what are the Diedrichs planning to do with their extra income? "I have a 24 year old son who just graduated with a degree in biology from U.C. Irvine. His dream has always been to go to medical school, but he's a single parent and simply can't afford it," say Monica. "I'm going to use the money I'm making to pay for his medical education. And then I'm going to make sure that both he and his brother attend the workshop and learn these strategies for themselves. They're both extremely bright, so I know if I can do it, so can they...with even better results."

Sincerely,
Monica and Albert Diedrich"

Now, a few questions:

- Do you think these students of mine could have made these outrageous profits in mutual funds?

- Have you made this much money in such a short time?

- Are your advisors making this kind of money?

- Do your advisors know about the methods which produce these kinds of results?

- Did you see one place where a student mentioned that my company or I received a percentage of their profits?

- Where are you going to go to learn these things? And, even if you paid thousands of dollars for a two-day workshop, would $300,000 in pure cash profits be worth it?

Does everyone make money following my formulas? I don't think so. But I can't find too many that have lost who practiced the strategies (my way) before using real money. From time to time the stock market has down time, or bumps and there always is a potential to lose a little. I say a little because you should only have small amounts at risk. Say $2,000 to $4,000 on a particular trade—even if you have hundreds of thousands to invest. You need to be right more than you are wrong.

FORMULAS—WHICH ONE?

I'll list some of my more widely-used formulas here. There are many combinations and variations on a theme. There are add-on strategies, and exit strategies if something goes wrong. These are designed for fun and profits. Fun, you ask? Well, I'm suggesting a minor lifestyle change here. If making money is not fun, then you won't stick with it and you won't get good at it.

FAMILY, FUN AND FINANCES

- Rolling Stocks
- Stock Splits
- Options (Buying Calls and Puts)
- Writing Covered Calls
- Selling Puts
- Bull Put Spreads
- Bull Call Spreads

- Turnarounds
- Spin-offs
- IPOs
- Bottom Fishing
- Rolling Options
- Range Riders

HOW TO USE THEM

Each one of these formulas is explained in more detail elsewhere. Some are covered extensively in a real, live "experiential" workshop. Here I will list a few generalized rules.

1. Each one is used at different points. The market (or a stock) is either going up, going down, or going sideways. Some of the preceding are used in those three areas.

2. Each formula has an exit—a time to get out, and back up exit points to minimize losses if the underlying stock movement is wrong.

3. These formulas can be used in tandem. For example, when a stock is going up, you can buy a call option, sell a put, do a bull call or bull put spread, or just buy the stock.

4. The rules for one formula do not necessarily apply to anothers. Each has a stand-alone set of characteristics.

5. You should know of all of these but get good at one at a time. Each takes practice.

These formulas are designed to add to your asset base and provide income for other things. One of the best pieces of advice I've ever received was to spend profits, not principal. A friend just received $80,000 in an insurance settlement. He asked my opinion.

"Put it to work," I said. "Don't spend it." Well after a new car, some presents, and a trip he had a little under $30,000 left. He put it in mutual funds. He's young, 25 or so, and I'll bet when he sees the dismal returns on his investments and grows tired of it, the money will come out of the mutual fund and be gone. This scenario is repeated continuously every day across this land.

One doctor took $70,000 and in one year after attending my workshop had over $2,000,000. Now spend some of those profits.

So what do you do?

1. Study the formulas before deciding which one you'll get good at–or become an expert in.

2. Decide how to deploy your money. This is based on your earning power, your cash needs, and your age.

3. Start paper/practice trading. There's a new book out by David Hebert called *On Track Investing*. It is all about paper trading, or Simutrading. It will really help you make more money and avoid losses. Call Origin Book Sales at 1-888-467-4446 or Wade Cook Seminars at 1-800-872-7411.

4. Choose a stockbroker who loves his job, knows options and spreads. At least get him a copy of this book or my other books. They think they know the strategies, but they just don't "get it."

5. Pick a small amount of money and go to work.

6. Constantly check results. Monitor your returns. Paper trade the stock or option.

7. Keep learning. Make education your way of life.

PAY THE BILLS

My style of investing is to use the market, specifically these formulas to generate extra cash profits. With this money we can live, pay our living expenses, and get out of debt. With some money we can start buying stocks, or real estate or whatever for the long run.

We can also go back to school, take courses, spend more time with the kids, and make bigger donations to churches and charities.

Ancient Wisdom

I don't want to end this chapter without putting in a plug for the Bible. It is the source for great formulas. I think God's rules should be first. We obey and we're happy, if we don't, we're unhappy. Life is pretty simple to me. Teach me the rules and I'll play your game.

Start with Leviticus 19. It's a great place to lay a foundation. Check out Psalms 119. Learn of Abraham's Covenant. Study Job, the Parable of the Ten Talents, the story of the Rich Young Ruler, and a host of others found all throughout the Bible.

Publisher's Note: The author has written several books on attributes of personal and business excellence. If you would like to expand your quest for success, pick up Business Buy The Bible, Don't Set Goals (the Old Way), *and* A+ *at a bookstore near you.*

Have a purpose in life,
and having it, throw into your work
such strength of mind and muscle as
God has given you.

Thomas Carlyle

CHAPTER 2

CASH FLOW, CASH FLOW, CASH FLOW

There are three reasons for investing–three benefits of owner-ship. These benefits are cash flow, tax write-offs, and growth. Usually we have to look at and buy three different types of invest-ment alternatives–each one produces a singular benefit to claim one of these three benefits.

Some investments produce more than one. For example, REIT or Real Estate Investment Trust may give off income, as hopefully the real estate owned by the trust is growing in value, and the tax deduction passes through the trust to the investor. Publicly traded limited partnerships may do the same thing. We know real estate owned outright may get these results.

If you want growth in stocks, you might have to give up large dividends or income from the company. Other stocks produce fair-ly nice dividends but grow very slowly. The question most financial professionals ask seems inappropriate. At best they bespeak a lazi-ness or unwillingness to help people get ahead. Here's their ques-tion: "Which one of these three is important to you?" Then they do their "asset allocation" thing and you are led to feel comfortable with their "computerized" plan for you. Let me be more specific. Your need for tax write-offs will change from year to year. Your need for growth or an increase in assets will increase as you get older. And this is funny because what do you need growth for, but to have assets to sell or hopefully produce income in the future? What a weird conundrum. Why aren't you learning how to invest in ways that produce cash flow now?

Your need for cash flow will be persistent and if you're like most people, your need for income will increase. I have not met one older or retired person who wants to cut back or lower their standard of living. Then why this fatalistic view? Why does so much garbage thinking cloud our decision-making process?

I'm appalled at the mental mindset of these so called "product salesmen." It's as if you have a nail and they have their one hammer to hit it. Your diverse problems don't matter. Their computer program will spit out the garbage that will cause you to think about and buy their recommended listing of boring products.

Cash Flow

Would it be considered true wealth if you have enough monthly income to live the way you want? This could be defined as the ability to travel, to donate more to your church, to be a great doting grandparent; to truly live? Then why all the investments that produce nothing for this lifestyle?

Also, I'm not sure many people want to really retire and do nothing. Their job, business, or career may have consumed them, but when they are ready to call one chapter of their life quits and retire, they still want to be busy and have challenges. They sure don't want the same 9 to 5, nor a life of nothing.

I've got the perfect solution. Use this time to manage your money, increase your income, and increase your lifestyle. Most businesses and even most types of real estate investing are too demanding and way too time consuming. Traditional stock market investing is too boring.

Let's try the stock market the Wade Cook way, with a small part of your money. Let's put it to work. Let's put your mind to work at least part-time and watch it grow–watch the cash come in.

I'd like to make a point before I go on. Your retirement age does not have to be when you're 65 or 70. How about 30 or 40, or even 25–as a young newlywed couple, ready to have babies. Once you learn these strategies, your time will be freed up.

It would be impossible now to tell you of all the thousands of people in their 20s and 30s who have quit their jobs and now use the stock market as a business. They do it my way. Their stories are heartwarming if not downright unbelievable. If I didn't hear these personally, or in their letters, I would have a hard time believing it too. I wish my misguided critics could read my mail just one day.

TREAT IT LIKE A BUSINESS

One continuous slogan has been to treat the stock market like a business. Before I answer how, let me tell you that "cash flowing" the stock market, or treating it as a business, part or full-time, should be considered by you as a new lifestyle. Why?

1. You can do it part or full-time. You control the hours.
2. It doesn't take a lot of money to get started. A few thousand dollars and you're ready to roll.
3. No employees, rent, insurance, or other business overhead.
4. You can use a spare bedroom or your car phone.
5. You can become a specialist in an area of interest to you.
6. It's easy to involve family members; even small children can participate.
7. You can quit, take time off, or vacation (and get to a phone) anytime you want.

So what is the Wade Cook way? Why is my system so different? It is not really different from the strategies the big guys use. It is vastly different than the way a typical stockbroker works and totally different than what a typical financial journalist or news pundit reports on or writes about.

How do you treat the stock market like a business? Well, it is surely not to be out of control of your money. I don't mean to turn your life over to someone who has only their commissions and management fees in mind. I do numerous radio and TV interviews. The announcers don't seem to get it. I have about 13 really good cash flow strategies. Each one has as an end product, the production of profits–or actual cash. This, you must know, is heresy in this arena. I'm glad I don't live in Salem, Massachusetts.

If you have a business, you move products or services out the door. Let's say you have a corner convenience store. You would not go to the wholesale warehouse and say, "Okay, I need a case of those potato chips, a box of pepperoni sticks, three cases of soda pop, a jar of pickles and I'm going to keep this stuff untill I'm 65." In fact, you judge your wholesale purchases on how fast things move. It is turnover and quick sales that generate profits.

Why, oh why with a part of your money don't you do the same thing? Now, I'm not going to leave you hanging because with all the brainwashing going on, you probably don't have a very good answer to that question. I use formulas that put the emphasis on selling, not buying. It's the exit that's profitable; not the entrance.

What is a formula? Call it a system, or a method. A formula is a complete A to Z (though most only have a few steps or components) modus operandi (MO) for generating profits. Now, when I say profits, I mean actual cash. Cash you can spend on groceries or mortgage payments or buy a new car.

Let me give you a quick example. A stock slams down, even on good earnings, then it backs off from $74 to $62. It finds support at $62 and starts back up. It may take three weeks to three months to get back in the $70s. We buy on the dip. Now to close the formula, we pick an exit point, we sell, make $4, and do it again tomorrow on a different stock. This is a formula. It generates cash quickly.

Now we can jazz it up, using 10 contracts as an example.

1. We could buy call options at the $60 or $65 strike price. A small move in the stock could be a terrific percentage move in the call option; $62 stock to $66, a $4 ($4,000) call option to $6.50–or $6,500–a $2,500 cash profit. It's not $4,000 profit as when we did the stock, but we only have $4,000 tied up and at risk to make $2,500 in profits.

2. We could sell a put–say the $60 put for $3, or $3,000. As the stock moves up, we could buy the put back at a lower price or let it expire and keep the $3,000.

3. We could do a $55/$60 bull put spread.

4. We could do a $55/$60 or $60/$65 bull call spread.

5. We could buy the stock on margin.

And we can blend these strategies and even do them in entities, like a pension type account, which pays no taxes. (Not all strategies are allowed to be done in tax-free entities.)

Do you see how exciting these formulas can be? This book is full of strategies or formulas for cash flow.

The formulas are understandable. Each one has a place–a time and a season. Each one generates income either now or in the future. Look at the following comparison:

THE WADE COOK METHOD	TRADITIONAL METHODS

1. Long-term hold
  a. Blue Chip Stocks
  b. Bargain Stocks
  c. Mutual Funds,
     REITS, et cetera.
	1. Long-term hold
	  a. Blue Chip Stocks
	  b. Bargain Stocks
	  c. Mutual Funds,
	  REITS, et cetera.

2. Rolling Stocks Buy and sell on repeated and predictable patterns (highs and lows).	
3. Options Proxy investing–options for safety investing.	
4. Writing Covered Calls Generate income monthly on stocks you own or buy.	
5. Stock Splits (and other news) There are five strategies to enter and exit stocks or options doing splits.	
6. Sell Puts Generate income–get paid now.	
7. Bull Put Spreads Generate income, limit risk, lessen margin.	
8. Bull Call Spreads Writing covered calls by covering with options.	
9. Bargain Hunting Bottom fishing for long-term hold or quick pops.	
10. Spin-offs Capture the stock–buy options on stock.	

THE WADE COOK METHOD	TRADITIONAL METHODS
11. IPOs If not at first, wait, get in, and out. Use 60 day IPO rule. 12. Turnarounds Catch the wave up and do stocks or proxy investing. 13. Slams and Peaks (Really two strategies.) Catch the turn one to five day plays. Quick cash. 14. Range Riders Buy and sell at tops and bottoms all the way up.	

I'll let this comparison do the talking. There's money to be made so let's get going. Stop listening to old, stale, and might I say risky advice. You see, by forcing the issue, (putting the emphasis on selling for cash flow), you have to do more homework. You invest for a certain reason. You put the emphasis on selling or closing out a position, not on buying. You buy so you have something to sell; there's a rhyme and a reason.

For most people reading this, buying and holding long-term is just wishful thinking. They need cash, and want more income. If I were teaching people with hundreds of thousands of dollars, maybe my seminars would more closely reflect the opinions of the big mutual fund guys. Bless their hearts, they're just out of contact and out of sync with the average American. They must think everyone has $1,000,000 or so. Some won't even talk to people with less than $25,000 to invest. But people with $2,000, $5,000 and $10,000 pile into my seminars. They want a way out. They're looking for help. Sure they wish they could put $100,000 into Disney, $200,000 into GE, $50,000 into Boeing and so on and so on. But they can't. While everyone else shuns them, I take them in. They can take their $2,000 and work a formula. It grows. They pay some bills. They make hundreds or thousands of dollars—and sometimes several thousand dollars a month. They could never generate this kind of cash flow with a mutual fund, or even a blue chip stock, as wonderful as those investments are for some people.

"I first heard about Wade Cook through an ad in our local paper for the Financial Clinic. We had 17 years investment experience prior to the Wall Street Workshop™, but decided that we might be able to do better by attending. Our favorite strategies are Covered Calls and Bull Put Spreads. Our goals and dreams for the money are to pay off some credit card debt, give more to our church, and live comfortably off the rest. Starting in December '98 and doing just six Covered Calls each month our base portfolio has increased 20% in value and our call premiums have been $4,500, $6,500, and $7,700 for rates of return 15, 22, and 26%. All this time we were able to help our youngest daughter and son-in-law on the down payment on their first home.

Donald and Joan Holiday"

The big guys are saying, "Hey Americans, you're not smart enough. You won't understand this stuff. Give us your money and we'll take care of it. Sure we'll charge fees, but you just let us take care of your money." Then along comes Wade Cook who says, "Hold it Americans. You *are* smart enough. You *can* understand these ways. You take control and make it happen. I'll be the icebreaker and cut up the ice, you follow in your kayak. I'll pioneer the way, figure it out and teach you." Thousands upon thousands have responded.

Ironically, one of my favorite formulas is buying stocks for the long term. You'd never know it by the comments in the press. To buy good solid stock in companies making big-time money is a mainstay of my portfolio and my seminars. It's a great way to go.

However, one of the weirdest things has happened. I've been criticized for the strangest thing. When I use the long-term hold method in my own portfolio, it has caused an adverse result in my company's financial statement. Let me give a more full explanation.

You will need these explanations because you too will get criticized by well meaning, but slightly off base people. Tell them you want more income. They will have to put up or shut up when you say, "I want to generate $6,000 a month of income." If they can't help you, read on or get to one of my workshops.

Note: We have a newsletter called EXPLANATIONS.
Call 1-800-872-7411 for a FREE copy, or to subscribe.

$804,000

Most of you know I'm CEO of a publicly traded company. We have to report everything in our SEC reports. Our brokerage account reports are a "snapshot" in time. A few years ago, with millions in our accounts, and making hundreds of thousands of dollars in realized profits, we had an unusual thing happen. At the end of the year, we had several positions (stocks) way down in value: Disney, Gillette, Boeing, et cetera. The stocks took a hit at the end of 1997. We showed an "unrealized loss" of $804,000. Of course, we didn't want it to happen, but they were down none the less. Just like most of you, we did not sell them. We waited for the stocks to rebound. The first quarter (three months) of the next year we were up $755,900 in realized and unrealized gains.

We've explained this to the news writers so many times, but to no avail. There is one man who writes for a particular large news agency that seems to have it out for me. Amid countless pieces of great information, he will find every picayune negative thing he can find. He ignores mountains of good news and writes extensively about molehills. For a year or so he mentions this $804,000 in about every article. It's annoying. I shouldn't wonder why, because negativism sells. What's odd is that we post all of our trades on an Internet site (wadecook.com). The whole world can see every trade. Oh, before I go on, this last year shows $837,000 real profits and unrealized gains. It's all in our SEC filings. Do you think he will get it? I doubt it. And just think, the $804,000 unrealized capital loss was on about $7,800,000 in the account. That's not bad in a horrible year-end like 1997 was. In 1997 we had the Asian Flu, and a South American mess, et cetera. Now, this $837,000 gain this past year was on about $2,800,000 in the account. You see, we took out millions to buy hotels and other investments. I think $837,000 on $2,800,000 is quite remarkable and commend our Trading Department. And you know 1998 was no picnic. Remember the

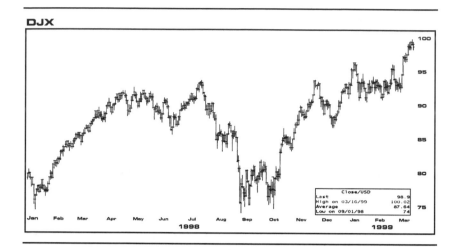

DJX

Close/USD
Last 98.9
High on 03/16/99 100.02
Average 87.64
Low on 09/01/98 74

Jan Feb Mar Apr May Jun Jul Aug Sep Oct Nov Dec Jan Feb Mar
1998 **1999**

summer to Oct/Nov time period? Look at the Dow for the whole year. Most funds and other investors just caught up to break even. We excelled.

Yes, we excelled, but you know what? We don't use these numbers in our advertisements. We teach the strategies. We don't make promises on returns. That is up to you and your broker.

How I would love to debate a strategy or formula with these people. Oh no, they just want to criticize anything they can find. Now the real irony is this, all of our cash flow formulas were making us lots of money. The only one that lost was the one all the other guys teach and use. The long term hold method was eating up our profits–although unrealized. It would be fun to see the articles read, "Wade Cook's 13 Cash Flow Formulas generate millions–the old tried and true formula, the ones the big boys use, has killed his profits."

So why do I bring this up? I do it for you. You, the person struggling to make ends meet. You, the rational person who needs an extra $600 to $2,000 per month. You the young mother who wants to stay home with your children. You, the overworked cab driver that needs more quality time, and you the American worker who wants to give and share more.

It's sad. Sad, because people read the negativism and then don't come to our events, or don't know what really works. Honestly, I feel I've created the first workshop that could easily cost you $100,000 or more to not attend. People read negative things and are blinded by the falsity. Everyone believes the accusations but not the denial. It is sad. I just wish these critics would really study and use these formulas before they speak out.

These formulas are workhorses. They have a beginning, middle, and an end. The emphasis is where it should be–*on results*.

All I want you to get out of this chapter is to know that formulas for cash flow exist. If you want more monthly income, the following chapters show you how. The process does require a small mindset change. You'll have to give up some old ways of thinking. You'll have to find a broker who is into "cash flow." You'll have to study and learn these formulas.

What is the trade off? Old "slow producing" stocks to new quicker cash flow formulas. ($20,000 should produce $2,000 to $6,000 per month, not $2,000 a year.) That's right! From now on we'll talk about two weeks or four weeks, good cash flow returns.

ROLLING STOCKS HERE AND NOW

Rolling stocks is still my first stock market love, but it's not my only love. For many beginners it is a great way to start. It's amazing the things people learn about the market, the companies, and about themselves as they employ these strategies.

Couple rolling stocks with other strategies like options and the chances of winning increase. Also, you can do option spreads on rolling stocks (bull put spreads, bear call spreads) and you can write covered calls on the stocks over $5 (if they have options).

Rolling stocks is the best bread and butter cash flow strategy in an otherwise crazy market.

UP, DOWN, OR SIDEWAYS

I think a fact that many people have come to realize is that the market, and every stock in the marketplace, is either going up, or it is going down, or it is going sideways.

Doing rolling stocks is a system of taking advantage of a side-ways movement in a stock price. We look at charts or watch stock prices. We notice support levels and resistance levels. We look for repeating patterns. We look for a channel. We observe and plan our entrance and exit points beforehand.

Look at the following five charts of rolling stocks. Obviously these were rolling at the time of this writing. They may not be rolling, or the prices (roll range) may have changed before you read this. Please check current prices, and roll ranges and then practice trade 15 to 20 times on various stocks before you use real money. Let your broker see these so he can get used to this strategy.

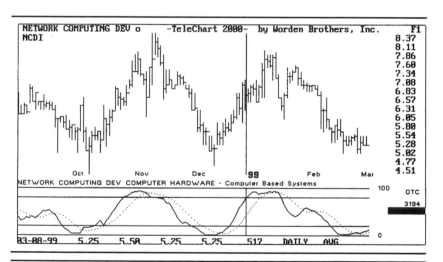

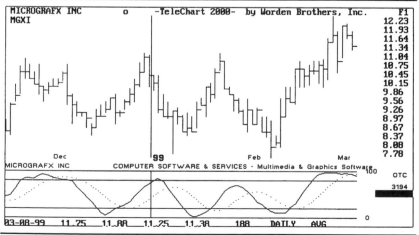

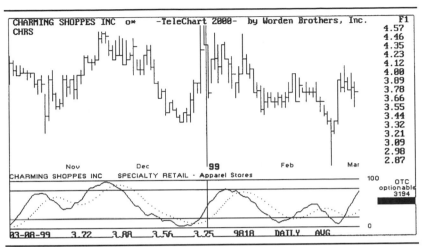

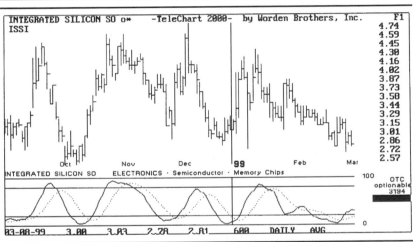

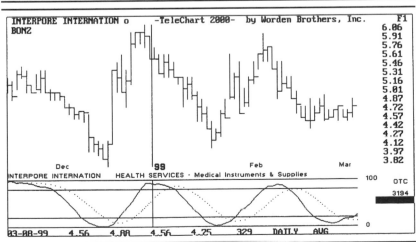

Another way to look at rolling stocks is to only buy (or own) them on their way up, and then don't own them on their way down.

Sometimes we don't buy the stock at the very bottom of its roll range. We also don't always sell at the very top or most opportune sell point. Remember to not get greedy. Don't glean the vineyard. You don't need to make every penny on every roll. In fact if you try to make $1.125 ($1⅛) on a 75¢ to $1 more predictable roll range, you'll lose out on many rolls. Your profits will increase as you take the shorter and quicker rolls.

PATTERNS

My years of investing have taught me many things. One is to get better at the power of observation. I watch these roll patterns carefully. I've seen three distinct patterns. They look like this:

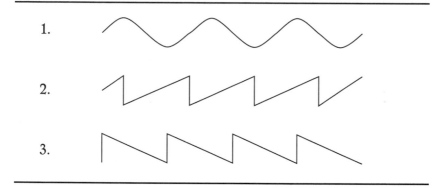

1. The roll is smooth. The pattern fairly consistent.
2. The stock price takes weeks or months to climb up to a certain point, then, wham, it comes down overnight.
3. The stock price spikes up then trickles down. Then it spikes up again.

MORE EXPENSIVE STOCKS

All we've looked at here so far has been lower priced stocks. I think anyone who has been in the market at least six months has noticed roll ranges on more expensive stocks. These rolling stocks get noticed, but we may have a hard time playing them as they are so expensive.

If the stock is rolling between $115 and $130, we can buy call options on the stock when the price is low and expected to go back up. Say it bounces off of $115 and is at $116, even after hitting $117 earlier in the morning. It starts up again. We could buy the $115 or $120 call out one to two months. As the stock gets to $126, we could sell those calls for a nice profit. And then buy the $130 or $125 puts as it falls.

These options give us a chance to play the better stocks with less money at risk. Don't ignore all the other rules of option investing (including controlling the risk) just because these roll patterns look so good. Be careful to choose the right strike prices and select the appropriate month for maximum protection even if you have to sacrifice some of your profits for safety's sake.

What we truly and earnestly aspire to be, that in some sense we are.—These mere aspirations, by changing the frame and spirit of the mind, for the moment realizes itself.

Anna Jameson

CHAPTER 3

OPTIONS FOR SAFETY

There are many books written on options. Many are very technical and hard to read. But they are widespread and should be read.

"Dear Wade,

I had the pleasure of attending your introductory seminar in New York this past Saturday. I was impressed. Given I have spent more than 30 years in the financial field, I have never seen such a well thought out, orchestrated, practical and successful approach to trading. Your "meter-drop," setting reasonable targets and stop-out points, are already turning my own financial world around.

To add some credibility to these observations, I operated a top quality futures fund, Group Veritas, in the Middle East during the early 90s. My books on trading options are in many investing libraries. The co-authored book with Dr. Andrew Rudd on Modern Portfolio Theory was required reading for many top quality MBA programs.

Thank you, again, for sharing your successful methods and for being the Christian businessman you are.

Cordially,
Henry Clasing"

I have written on options extensively in *Wall Street Money Machine* and *Stock Market Miracles*. There are new chapters on spreads created with options in this book. Most stockbrokers know the basics of option investing. Others know very little. Because of the magnified movement of option prices based on an underlying movement in a stock, the profit potential of options with small amounts of money can be immense and should be studied.

All I can do here is put out information—my take, if you will, that will help you see options in their proper light. First I'll wax philosophical. Options, the word has the same root word as optimism. They can add much excitement once you know how to use them. Once understood you will be happy to make options your friend. As in life, one can be optimistic when they have many options.

OPTIONS AS A SAFETY HEDGE

It's difficult to imagine an investment with an expiration date as a safe investment. While not totally safe, they do provide an amount of safety—more so than a typical stock investment in some ways. Let's say your broker puts you into a $60 stock. What's your downside? It's zero, or a potential $60 loss. If you own a $60 call, you purchased for $4, which gives you the right to buy the stock at $60 for a month or two, your downside is the $4.

Options are in 100-share increments, so one contract would be $400. Four hundred dollars locks down 100 shares at the $60 price. If the stock moves up $3 to $5, your option could go to $6 or $7. Sell it anytime before the third Friday of expiration month and you take in $700 (in this example). That's a $300 profit on your $400 investment.

If the stock goes down you could lose big time, 100 shares at $60 is $6,000. If the stock drops to $40, you've lost $2,000. Yes, your option is also down and may not recover. You would be out $400, not $2,000. You see, in this example options are better than stocks. If the stock goes way up, to say, $92, your option would fly up also. Think, if you have the right to buy a stock at $60 and the stock is at $92, your option could be worth at least $32, and more if there's still time left. Remember that part of the premium you pay, and receive when you sell is the time value left before expiration. Now $6,000 could become $9,200, a nice move. But $400 is now $3,200 or more. This is better in that you have so little cash tied up–or at risk.

Stocks are great investments if they are bought right. So are options, so don't bad mouth options until you've walked a mile in their shoes. Don't be critical until you've had the magnified option profits and see how they limit downside risk. Tell me, what other investment has limited downside risk and unlimited upside potential?

SPECIFIC TIMES

I like options when used in conjunction with other complete formulas. For example, I like rolling stocks. (See my book *Wall Street Money Machine.*) We usually do rolling stocks with less expensive stocks, say in the $1 to $8 range. But many $120, $180, and $240 stocks roll between price points–support at the bottom, resistance at the top. They roll in nice patterns.

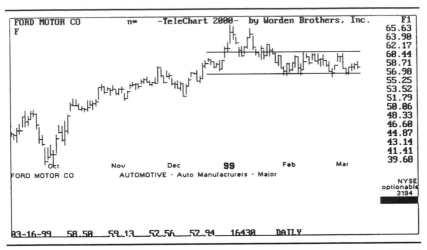

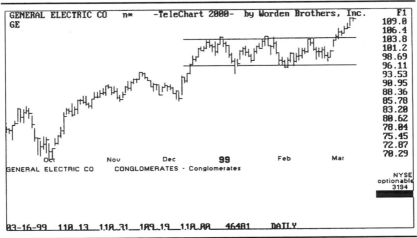

What about rolling options? Here's how it works. A stock is rolling from $130 to $140. The rolls are not perfect, but when the stock gets in the low $130s or high $120s it mills around for a week and heads back up. It usually takes three to four weeks to get to the high $130s. Once in a while it bumps against $140. When it's low we could buy a one or two month out $130 call. Let's look:

STOCK	$130 CALL OPTION
$132	$5.00
$134	$6.00
$136	$7.50
$138	$9.25
$140	$11.25

We'll buy 10 contracts for this example. Ten $5 option contracts equal $5,000 and we control 1,000 shares at $130. Remember we're not buying options to buy the stock. We're buying options to wait for an increase in value then we sell at a profit. We could sell all or part of these contracts in a week at $7.50 and pocket $2,500 profit on our $5,000 investment. Yes, we could lose all or part of the $5,000, so we should only use risk money. Track plays like this on paper first.

Also, let's increase our power of observation. What if it gaps up? What if the company announces great earnings? What if there's a share buyback or stock split announcement? If it goes to $150 you could make a really nice profit. Sometimes we sell at the $7.50 or $9 price, and even though we have made a profit, we lose out on the additional increase. Oh, well–be happy. ($2,500 or $4,000 profit is not bad for two hours or two weeks.)

Now with the stock at $140 or so you could buy a put option as it comes back down.

STOCK	$135 PUT OPTION
$140	$2
$136	$4
$134	$5
$132	$6

Are you seeing the potential plays? Buy for $2,000 and sell for $5,000. If the stock rises we could lose our $2,000. This put play brings up our next "safety first" option play.

PUTS FOR SAFETY

Put option values go up as stocks go down. Let's say you have a great stock. You want to keep it. It has had an awesome run up of late from $60 to $85. It might go higher but the news has played out. You don't want to sell but you also don't want to lose value. With the stock at a high of $85 why not buy a put to protect the downside. If $85 is a new high and you don't think the price can be sustained buy the $85 put or the $80 put. As the stock moves down your put goes up in value—compensating for any loss in the stock.

STOCK	$80 PUT OPTION
$85	$2.00
$80	$4.50
$76	$7.00
$72	$10.00
$65	$17.00

If this stock falls out of bed, you could sell the put and buy calls if you think it's going up. That $2 premium will be just wasted insurance money if the stock goes up or stays up near the $85 price.

I keep getting my digs in at our so-called professionals. Don't you think they should have shown you this? The huge fund managers and billion-dollar investors use puts all the time as a hedge. I guess you have to decide whose cab you want to be in.

STOCK SPLITS

There are companies announcing stock splits all the time. They split their stocks to make their shares more affordable or to increase their float of stock. Sometimes greed sets in, hi-tech company Board of Directors see all of their competitors splitting their stocks, and they jump in. I like stock splits. I've seen so many stocks go from $90

STOCK SPLITS – FIVE TIMES

TIME	STRATEGY
1. PRE-ANNOUNCEMENT a. They run in groups. b. They historically split at certain times or prices. c. They have a shareholders meeting to authorize more stock (usually for a split). d. Other news.	• Buy at the money calls, buy slightly out of the money calls. • Sell puts at certain times for prices. • Watch for roll ranges. • Probably do options with expiration dates after the split date.
2. ON THE ANNOUNCEMENT, BE CAREFUL a. Stocks spike up. b. If you don't catch it within seconds, wait for #3. c. This is my least favorite. The stock and options are too volatile.	• Watch out. Options rise dramatically. If you chase it you'll get burned. • Don't place market orders – only place limit orders. • If option spikes up, consider sitting it out. Wait for a better play.
3. BETWEEN ANNOUNCEMENT AND THE SPLIT DATE a. Wait a few hours or days after the announcement. b. This time is usually four to six weeks. c. Many stocks roll up and down based on other news.	• Give options a chance to settle down. • Watch for roll patterns. • If the stock has had a quick run up it may back off. Look for other news.

4. INTO THE SPLIT

a. Many stocks pull back the week of the split, but by Friday (split date), it runs up.

b. Many stocks fall several dollars after split – Monday following Friday split.

- Buy call options, sell put option into split. Say Wednesday then sell Friday (Ex-dividend date is Monday).

- Sell everything.

- Buy again in #5.

5. AFTER THE SPLIT

a. Wait a few days.

b. Many stocks lull around for a few weeks, or months. Wait for news sometime as we head into the next quarter

- Consider buying put on split date.

- Look for roll patterns.

- Consider LEAPS® if you like the stock. Buy on dips.

down to $45 on a 2:1 split and go back up to around $90 within six to 12 months. I've challenged people everywhere to find a company that has done a split where the stock is not back to the original price in three to four years. "You can probably find a few," I say, "but if you find one I'll show you 50 that have gone back up within a year." Yes, that's a doubling of your money.

Once again though, what if you want to play these splits but you have limited resources? You can play options on the stock. There are five times to play these splits and dozens of micro-times within these five. Before I list the five I hope you've read between the lines and figured this out that if there are five times to get in there must be five times to get out. Don't ever go in the entrance until you know your exit. Again, to a different tune, once you know your exit, and only then, should you go in.

Do your own homework. Chart your own stock, practice, observe, and practice.

THE OPTIONS SPLIT

When the stock splits the options split, and so does the option cost basis. If you purchase 10 contracts at $6, or $6,000 on an $80 stock doing a 2:1 split; after the split you'll have 20 contracts with a cost basis of $3 on a $40 call strike price. Again, leverage at its best.

Now, back to #4. I said sell everything. That's what I do, except for LEAPS® on my better high flying stocks. Too many times the stocks dip right at the split date. Think, if there is a magnified movement in the option and the stock goes down, the option might not recover before the expiration date. You can watch me do this on W.I.N.™ (at wadecook.com).

Example: I really like Dell Computer (DELL), but even DELL has certain volatility. On Friday March 5th, Dell was around $84. It split and on Monday opened up at $43 (or $86 pre-split price). It rose to $45, plus change by Tuesday. When it was at $45 I bought the March $42.50 puts for .75¢. Two days later I sold these same options for $1\frac{1}{8}$ or $1.125. I did 50 contracts so I made $\frac{3}{8}$ or $37.50 times 50 or $1,750 minus a few hundred for commissions. A day later these same options were going for almost $2 on a stock dip to 41^{11}/_{16}$. I'm happy with my meter drop profit of $1,750 for a few days.

OPTIONS FOR THE LONG TERM

LEAPS® arc calls and puts that can be purchased or sold out one and two years. LEAPS® are written in July for $2\frac{1}{2}$ years out. In July, the next January LEAPS® just become the January options.

I've been teaching a strategy for years and many people have made tens of thousands of dollars, even hundreds of thousands of dollars. One example I use is on Microsoft, another is DELL. Other companies might work as well.

At the time this book was being written, Microsoft was around $160. Microsoft has a history of stocks splits every 15 months or so. To make this work we need to make some assumptions; simply that Microsoft will just keep doing what it has been doing: making money and doing stock splits. That's all, and there is no guarantee that it will do either. But, you know what? Sometimes it's just fun to surmise–to say "what if?"

The $200 call LEAPS® for the year 2001 were going for $26 each. That's $26,000 to control 1,000 shares of Microsoft. Stop right there and ask yourself; How do I like locking down a $200 price on Microsoft for the next two years? And, is this risk money? If it doesn't perform; if the stock goes down I'll lose $26,000. Is this risk worth it? Read on.

Step 1: We spend $26,000 and control 1,000 shares of Microsoft at the $200 strike price.

Step 2: Microsoft announces a stock split–okay they made the announcement at the end of January, 1999. The stock moved up to $170. As we were going to press with this book the stock had fallen back to $145 and was back up to around $165.

Step 3: The stock splits, say when it hits $170 to two shares at $85. Our options split. We now have 20 contracts at a $100 strike price. That's the right to buy 2,000 shares of Microsoft at $100 for about 20 more months.

Step 4: The stock goes up to $110 to $140 in the next year.

Step 5: Microsoft announces another split in the spring/summer of the year 2000. The stock rises to $160 and splits to two shares at $80. Our options are now the $50 call strike price, and we own 40 contracts, or the right to by 4,000 shares of Microsoft at $50. If throughout the year 2000 the stock goes back up to $150 or so (let's forget the time value to the premium) and if we have the right to buy the stock at $50, our right, our option would be worth $100. That's $100 of intrinsic value. Sell them even a few minutes before the market close on the third Friday of January, 2001 and pocket $400,000 of profit. Real cash. Buy a house, get out of debt, or go to more movies. That's 40 contracts we sell for $100 each (4,000 times $100 is $400,000).

I know this is a lot of surmising, but look at Microsoft's track record, and DELL LEAPS® are even more exciting! I won't list the steps here. You figure it out. It's spectacular.

Okay, what if you don't have $26,000; then scrape together $2,600 and buy one contract. If it all pans out, that is a $40,000 profit. That's a $37,400 net profit. Enough to pay for some college tuition. Now, all you wet blankets throw some water on it. The downside is your options money. The upside is fantastic. We don't need Microsoft to do anything spectacular–just keep on keeping on. Do their thing. I'll go along for the ride.

Oh, I walk the walk. I have hundreds of contracts of Microsoft, DELL, IBM and Intel–not just 10. Yes you can write calendar spreads against these positions to generate income, but why? Who wants to get called out? Do spreads, write covered calls on other more steady stocks. We could buy the Microsoft stock itself if you don't like options that expire. That's $160,000 for 1,000 shares. On margin that's $80,000 (and you have to pay margin interest). Stocks are still a great way to go, but by buying these options you've tapped into a form of leverage. Even if we're only half-right the $26,000 could become $200,000 in two years. You've got to at least paper trade this one. Options for safety, for leverage, for excitement.

Practice, Study, and Practice

If you want to succeed in the world
you must make your own
opportunities as you go on.
The man who waits for some seventh
wave to toss him on dry land will find
that the seventh wave is a long time a
coming. You can commit no greater
folly than to sit by the roadside until
some one comes along and invites
you to ride with him to wealth or
influence.

John B. Gough

CHAPTER 4

MAKING WISE CHOICES

Each stock market formula we use is like a tool in the tool-box. Some are versatile and some are for a specific use. Like any good mechanic, you must know the particular or varied uses, the strengths and weaknesses of each tool.

This chapter will accomplish a monumental task. We will cross-examine the use of the formulas with a more traditional look at valu-ing stock and making smarter trades. We'll take a look at Fundamental Analysis, Technical Analysis, and Other Motivating Factors (OMFs).

A FUNDAMENTAL APPROACH

For years I've sided with the fundamental crowd, but now I see more of my entrance and exit points based on a technical approach–though my technical buy and sell thoughts are more intuitive than pure technical analysis. Let's cover fundamental analysis first. Fundamental analysis is a way, or several ways, to measure value. It looks at the things that are inherent to the company. It helps us see if the company is good or bad, if it is growing or not. It helps us compare companies to help determine a comparative value.

Fundamental analysis has set formulas for comparison. We can compare one bank stock to other bank stocks. We can compare a hi tech company to the other stocks in its sector or to the market as a whole. The most common component is the P/E, or price/earnings ratio. I could give the formula, but anyone can do that. Only I though can give you the cab driver's take on it, and make it simple— a stock may be at $125 and have a P/E of 32. Another stock may be $8 and have a P/E of 604. The P/E shows how much money you will pay to get at $1 of the company's earnings. In the first case $32 would buy $1 of earnings. ($604 in our next example buys $1 of earnings, even though the stock is only $8.) A typical NYSE company has average P/Es of 19.6 or sometimes 19.1 or 20.2. This is not a bad benchmark. In theory, the lower the P/E number the better. Nowadays, some Internet companies are trading at a 2,000 or a 3,000 P/E.

One caution, when you get the P/E you don't necessarily know if it's past tense, or trailing earnings; or future tense, or projected earnings, or a blend. Projected earnings are someone's guess at what the company will earn over the next year. The projected earnings are usually higher than what happened last year so the P/E will be lower. You see a lot of people who like low P/Es. You are buying the future earnings if you buy the stock today, but it's also more honest to look at what the company has done in the past. A blended P/E would give us the best of both worlds. I like it best when the company—or a news article—bases their P/E on six months back and six months forward. This is the best of both worlds. It is a better reflection of where the company really stands.

Each newspaper, magazine, analyst, and brokerage firm uses different time periods. It does get confusing. Just ask them or figure out what they base their P/Es on—more specifically what time periods they use. If you don't know, you could base selling or buying decisions on erroneous or incomplete information. Say a company has a trailing P/E (12 months) of 44 and an estimated P/E of 26. They tout the 26 and while it may happen—it may be 26 next year—it's a projection, a guess. Just be careful.

I think earnings are a key to stock movements. I've shouted it from the rooftops. Follow earnings, follow earnings. Is the company profitable? Are they (and the earnings) expanding or contracting?

Are their sales growing? What are they doing with their money? Are earnings growing because they've acquired another company? Will this acquisition slow them down? Are earnings growing from cost cuttings (sometimes good, or can contraction be bad?). Learn everything you can about a company's earnings.

Other ways to look at a company is its debt load. Is it excessive? Can it be managed? Debt is a killer of businesses. Debt should be manageable. Debt should not cause insolvency. Benchmark ratios vary from industry to industry, but I look for 30% or less of debt. That's 30% of the market capitalization. If the market cap is $600,000,000 then it should have less than $180,000,000 of debt. If the debt is over 50% and gets close to 70%, watch out. Debt is sometimes temporary. Look at how well the company has handled debt–both large and small–in the past.

Some people look at yields or dividend payouts. This is important if you're investing for this type of income. Most companies don't pay out large dividends and sometimes dividends are paid out of savings, et ceterea, just to keep up the dividend, even though the company is making no money. Looking at dividends or yields is becoming less and less important to many Americans.

Other people measure a return on equity–divide the after-tax profits by the book value to see how well the company is performing on its assets.

Another one I like is the book value–or breakup value measurement. Simply put, this is the value of a company's components compared to the market capitalization of the stock. Market cap is figured by taking all the outstanding shares and multiplying this number by the price of the stock.

$$\begin{array}{r} 100,000,000 \text{ shares} \\ \underline{x \quad \$23 \text{ (stock price)}} \\ \$230,000,000 \text{ Market Capitalization} \end{array}$$

Some great companies don't have great book values. What do you say about a Microsoft with a $250 billion market cap and a relatively small book value? It is a cash flow machine. People buy it for its earnings. Book value is a good measurement to make sure you are not overpaying for the stock. It also gives us a chance to buy under-valued stocks.

Some companies, more bread and butter types, trade at low book values. Remember when the Mexican peso was devalued? One company, which was trading at $16, dropped to $4. Its book value was $6 per share. It was undervalued. I bought at $4.50 and sold around $7 a few months later. Even today you can find companies with low book value compared to their stock price.

Bank stocks sometimes are down around their book value or loan portfolio value, and become takeover or merger candidates. Oil stocks and paper product stocks sometimes give one a chance to buy the assets at a discount.

All of these ways to value companies are important. They should be kept in perspective and be the tools we use for comparison purposes. They are good as a group to help us make decisions based on contrasting opinions.

TECHNICAL VIEWPOINTS

Technical analysis uses numbers to help us determine movements. These technical measurements help show when a stock will turn up, or go higher, when a stock will decline, die or turn around.

This study uses moving averages to show when a stock gets in a buy or sell range. Other technical viewpoints use call and put volume increases. Some technical analysts like gaps, when a stock price gaps up or down–to show the direction it will go thereafter. Others use money flows to see if money is entering the stock or leaving. There are many more including some way-out planetary models. A fun technical is when the NFC or AFC wins the super bowl. The market goes up or down, so they say.

Many people, like me, are busy. I know of these measuring sticks and I have three good stockbrokers who love the technical aspects of all this. I listen and use their advice sometimes. I'll say, "I want to buy 200 shares of Microsoft." They'll say, "Wait one or two days, it should drop a dollar or two." I question and get an ear full. I wait. They are often right. But Microsoft at $150 instead of $148 is not a big difference if it does a split and you sell 400 shares at $110 a few months later. That's a $16,000 profit. At $148 I would have made an extra $400. Like I said—not a big deal, sometimes.

Now when it comes to option trading—especially quick turn trades—every dollar is important. Technical analysis tells us when to get in and when to get out. Let's spell it "technEEcal" analysis. The "EE" are for Entrance and Exit points.

OTHER MOTIVATING FACTORS

Now the fun begins. Once we start to use fundamental aspects and technical entrance and exit points, then we realize that newsy items or other motivating factors also drive the stock or option.

Let's look at a "news announcement game" many companies play. For example, before the earnings announcement many companies downplay their earnings forecast. Many analysts say the earnings will be 92¢ per share. A week or two before June 30. (Note: We have four quarters a year, actually three plus the year-end report to drive the stock up or down. This gives us four newsy type reporting periods.) A company spokesman says that the earnings probably won't be that high. They adjust their forecasts, to say 78¢. Then the stock sometimes goes down—from $68 to $61. Then, voila, a few weeks later the actual earnings are reported at 87¢, a good 10% above forecasts. This process is almost comical. If this game weren't so common I wouldn't bring it up. We need to temper the news the company puts out with a dose of reality. And then after these adjusted reports are given they say we probably won't make that much next quarter, or next year. And with each announcement, or right before it, there's a whole lot of buying and selling going on. We as the little guy are always getting the short end of the stick. We jump in too late, and react after the play is over. Here's a thought: Watch for these pre-earnings announcements, wait for the dip, and then get in with stock or options. Practice this first.

In short, earnings reports drive stock up and down. So do anticipation of good or bad news. Watch for patterns. Look for good buying opportunities. Those buying opportunities are not when a stock peaks out or when it's on a new high. Let's look at this three month cycle; June 30th, a quarter end. A lot of newsy type announcements or projections come out around the 15th or so. Watch for these.

Now, remember the company has 45 days, or until August 15th to file its 10Qs, or SEC filings. In July the talk starts the whisper numbers, and such. Rumors, surmising, preannouncements of splits, share buy backs, et cetera. News abounds. We buy on rumors and sell on news (facts). I can't say how many times the actual filings are even better than expected and the stock falls from $82 to $78 and everyone scratches their heads. Why are we amazed when so many people know what the numbers will actually be? The stock went from $82 to $92 in the two to three weeks before the filing. The players are in and out when the filings are done. Knowing this, we won't get caught in the quarterly trap and go down in flames.

Now here's another problem, or opportunity, depending on how you look at it.

Sometimes crazily. A company has a great announcement but the stock goes down. A share buyback announcement is usually a good thing for the stock. The company is entering the market place to boost its stock, to dry up the supply or just to acquire the stock because they feel it's a good value.

Spin-offs and IPOs are news events. So are mergers, takeovers, and stock splits. Lawsuits–either instituted or ended–play into the picture, as does a management change.

All of these and more are called OMFs or the Other Motivating Factors. Most good news plays out in hours or a few days. Bad news seems to linger for months. Remember, get in the way of progress. Now, let's put this all together.

Fundamental analysis	helps us know	WHAT to buy or sell
Technical analysis	helps us know	WHEN to buy or sell
OMFs	help us know	WHY NOW to buy or sell

That's it. Use all three. Don't ignore any of this. With the use of all three methods, you'll make better and quicker decisions. Your cash profits should take off.

CHAPTER 5

DIVERSIFICATION: VARIATIONS ON A THEME

No, this chapter is not about mutual funds. What little I do say about them will not be too pleasant. This is diversification the Wade Cook way.

The old way of thinking is to diversify into various stock positions or buy mutual funds. The new way is to diversify your formulas. We're after cash flow, tax write-offs, and growth. Then use my cash flow formulas to produce profits to buy these other types of investments which will produce the benefits you want.

Each strategy not only has its own set of rules; and each formula not only has its own place, or time to be used, but each strategy has its own risk/reward ratio. Now, the formula you use depends on you. I know that sounds cliché, but don't let anyone sell you any investment until you know what MO (modus operandi) you're using. At least know where your back door is.

Mutual Funds

I'm not fond of mutual funds. Here's why:

1. Many of them own the same stocks. In fact, a large common group of stocks is owned pervasively by the larger funds. If there's a panic the exit will get crowded and prices will plummet. They all went in the door one at a time, but selling simultaneously could cause a problem.

2. Many no longer invest in what they promised. The brochures still say they do, but the makeup of the funds change. Managers may come or go, and change the style of the fund. What you think you're getting is not always the truth. Look at the following style drift charts. These scare me.

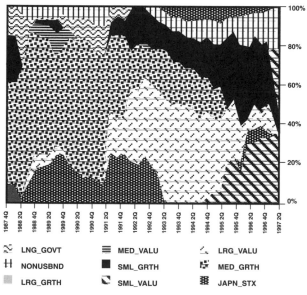

Style Drift Over Time
Fidelity Group
Fidelity Magellan(MF)

Style Drift Over Time
AIM Family of Funds
AIM Value(MF)

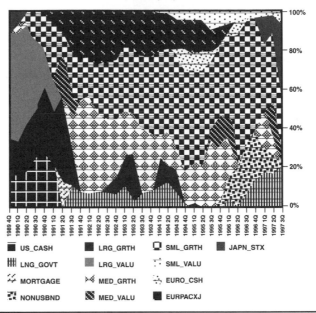

▦ US_CASH	▦ LRG_GRTH	▦ SML_GRTH	▦ JAPN_STX
▦ LNG_GOVT	▦ LRG_VALU	▦ SML_VALU	
▦ MORTGAGE	▦ MED_GRTH	▦ EURO_CSH	
▦ NONUSBND	▦ MED_VALU	▦ EURPACXJ	

Style Drift Over Time
Fidelity Advisor Funds
Fidelity Adv Growth Opp T(MF)

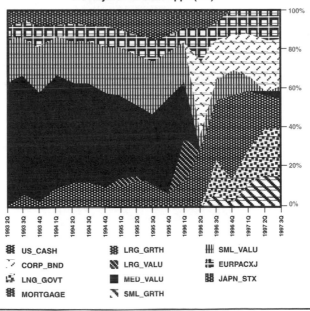

▦ US_CASH	▦ LRG_GRTH	▦ SML_VALU
▦ CORP_BND	▦ LRG_VALU	▦ EURPACXJ
▦ LNG_GOVT	▦ MED_VALU	▦ JAPN_STX
▦ MORTGAGE	▦ SML_GRTH	

If you want income from bonds and your fund now owns small start-ups, or IPOs that pay no dividends, you'll be displeased.

3.   Mutual funds came into existence to help people diversify and not have to choose which stocks to buy, as there were so many stocks available to make simple choices. It seems there are as many funds today as there were stocks when the mutual funds first started.

4.   I don't like the expenses of the funds (most are hidden and you get charged at the end of the year).

5.   I think the average person can pick stocks just as well as the big boys, once they know how.

In short, there are better ways to go.

Awhile ago, I heard an astonishing set of numbers. My stock-broker told me this, I don't have the actual numbers in front of me, and he lost the article. So, don't quote me on these numbers. He said something like this: of the 500 companies in the S&P 500, 37 of them make up 53% of the market capitalization of the group.

This is an incredible number. If true, a huge amount of wealth is owned in very few hands. In a way it's scary. What if a few of these drop in value? What if a sector (say hi-tech) gets hit? What if this small group is trading at really high multiples? These questions, and the exposure to risks, are real.

So here's what I did. I asked our trading department to "check this out." Here is a brief report of what they found out. Once you read this you'll have to decide a few things. Do you go along with the big boys? Do you buy mutual funds? Do you go off on your own and choose the big stocks or buy other stocks, not so big? Is there safety or danger in numbers?

REPORT FROM OUR RESEARCH AND TRADING

Never Has So Much Been Gained by So Few

You may have heard many times on various financial network shows how the market is being led by a small group of stocks.

Notable financial money manager James Cramer of the Internet site thestreet.com has pegged these stocks as TSELs–The Stocks Everyone Loves. According to a recent report a couple of our brokers have received from the large mutual fund group Putnam, these claims appear to be the case.

"Never have I seen in all my years in this business a year in which the market was led by such a small amount of stocks! Could you have done well this year? Yeah, if you picked the right stocks." These comments aren't exactly word for word how he said it, but they are very close. Our broker made these comments after reading a letter from Putnam in which they analyzed the percentage returns of both the Standard & Poor's 500 Index and the NASDAQ Composite Index for last year, 1998. This report then broke down which stocks were largely responsible for these returns. Actually they evaluated what these indexes returns would have been without certain stocks. The study performed by Putnam has revealed some pretty amazing results concerning the returns of both these indexes.

The Standard & Poor's 500 Index had a return of 28.72% last year. This may be deemed a pretty decent return on your money. Now, take a look further into the analysis of what the top 10 stocks in the index meant to the bottom line. They found that when they took out Microsoft Corp. (MSFT) the return of the index dropped about 4% to 24.73%. Take out this stock along with these next four stocks, General Electric Co. (GE), Intel Corp. (INTC), Wal-Mart Stores Inc. (WMT), and Exxon Corp. (XON) and the return drops a little over 9% to 19.62%. They continued on by taking out not only these five stocks, but also another five stocks, which were International Business Machines Corp. (IBM), Merck & Co. Inc. (MRK), Coca-Cola Company (KO), Cisco Systems Inc. (CSCO), and AT&T Corp. (T). The result for the S&P 500 then dropped almost 14% to a 14.99% return. You may be asking, why these 10 stocks? Out of the 500 stocks that make up this index these 10 are the ones with the largest member weightings, meaning they have the top 10 percentages of ownership. Microsoft Corp. (MSFT) is the number one stock on the list with percentage weighting (ownership) of 3.831%.

Putnam then did this type of analysis on the NASDAQ Composite Index. This index for 1998 generated a 39.63% return. This index based on these numbers outperformed the S&P 500 Index. Watch what happens though, when they take out the top 10 member weighting stocks in this index, starting with the number one stock, Microsoft Corp. (MSFT). Without Microsoft Corp. (MSFT) alone the NASDAQ Composite Index drops almost 16% to a return of 23.73%. Take out this stock along with the next four, Intel Corp. (INTC), Cisco Systems Inc. (CSCO), MCI/WorldCom Inc. (WCOM), and Dell Computer Corp. (DELL) and the return drops significantly to a -7.03%. This is not a typo! That is a minus sign. The return would have been a -7.03%. Take out these five stocks along with these next five, Oracle Corp. (ORCL), Sun Microsystems Inc. (SUNW), Amgen Inc. (AMGN), Tele-Communications Inc. (TCOMA) and Yahoo! Inc. (YHOO) and you would have had a -17.57% return.

What is the purpose of all this data? I guess it's to show how narrowly based this market's performance was, (and is?). This goes back to one of our brokers' earlier comments about whether anyone could have done well this year and the answer being, if you were in the right stocks. Our other broker within the same office said to me that he and other money managers are evaluated on their performance versus the S&P 500. They are trying to beat it. Based on valuations of these aforementioned stocks, a lot of professionals would believe some are overvalued. Wade Cook writes in *Stock Market Miracles* that the average P/E ratio on stocks on the New York Stock Exchange is about 20 and stocks on the NASDAQ is about 40. Dell Computer Corp. (DELL) has a current P/E ratio of 75. It seems what investors are saying when they buy is that they are willing to pay 75 times earnings for the stock. Let's just say for example, this company earns $100,000 for the year. Investors are willing to pay $7,500,000 for a company earning $100,000 a year. This is not the actual earnings for Dell. I just used their current P/E for illustrative purposes. Compare this earnings multiple to that of Cisco Systems Inc. (CSCO) whose P/E is 86 or Yahoo! Inc. (YHOO) whose P/E is 598. These multiples may be deemed too high for many price and valuation models for seasoned professionals. Now comes the "catch 22" these money managers now face.

In further discussing this observation with our broker he had made the comment it seems that times are changing, because now it seems money managers are evaluating their returns compared to the S&P not so much by whether they beat it. Let me one more time refer to the statement by our broker that you could have done well with the right stocks. Looking at the results of the Putnam research, the right stocks seemed to have been a select few. It seems that if your money managers didn't own these 15 to 17 stocks, they didn't compare with either of these indexes. In order for money managers to compare they pretty much had to own these same stocks, and had to probably buy them at higher multiples than they would've preferred. This broker continued to say that a lot of the clients just want to make money and if money managers didn't compare or make money along the likes of these indexes, jobs would be lost. Here's an observation gathered off of this information. When these professionals buy a more fairly valued stock, one that seems to be at the average P/E of 20 to 40 times earnings or better, their returns may not fare as well as the S&P 500 or the NASDAQ Composite. This may be because their stock choices are different from some of the ones mentioned previously. Hence, the possible risk of getting fired. My comment to the broker was, "It seems that if you guys want to compete and/or compare to these indexes, instead of trying to beat them, you're going to have to join them." Our broker said that for right now, "Don't try to fight it." Maybe he was talking to himself as well, when he made that statement.

Now that we have all been enlightened, we should consider taking heed to our brokers' words and not try to fight this rationale. Just be aware that this seems to be the environment in which we are investing.

This is the type of information we put on W.I.N.™ all the time. W.I.N.™ is a great resource wherein I post real trades for my subscribers to read. It's great tutorial information because you can look over the shoulder of people who trade and make money in the stock market everyday. You'll see trades not only from me, but also from my Team Wall Street instructors.

If you call now and mention this book, I'll make you a special introductory offer–five days of W.I.N.™ for only $10. That's five days full of trades, plus access to our great research sections and the journal of trades, which shows you what we've been doing for the last few months. Don't miss out. Call 1-800-872-7411 today.

SPiDeRs or SPDRs

Standard and Poor's Depository Receipts are a way to diversify in many stocks. These trade on the American Stock Exchange. SPDRs are trusts, which own stock in big companies. One of the large trusts–the S&P 500 Trusts–trade under the ticker symbol SPY.

Here's how it works. This is a trust set up to own all of the stocks, on a weighted basis, of the S&P 500. That's the 500 largest companies in the country. The stock in the trust trades for one-tenth (plus change) of the S&P 500 index, ticker SPX. If the index is at 1016, SPY will be going for 101.65 or so. It basically mirrors the SPX. The trust owns the stock and passes on the dividends from each company of the 500 companies which pay dividends.

I own a lot of these and am constantly having these small dividend amounts bombard my account. If you think the S&P 500 are

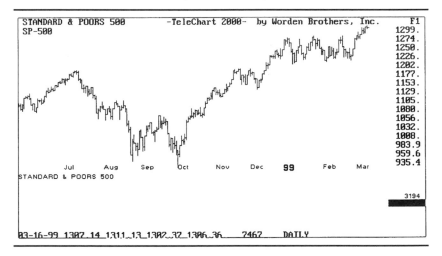

going up then buy the stock in this trust. If down, sell them. I think SPY is a good barometer on America. SPY is a good place to park cash if you are bullish on America. SPY can be bought on margin but there are no options on it. Also watch this stock as the market rolls. There are many buying opportunities. Look at the charts.

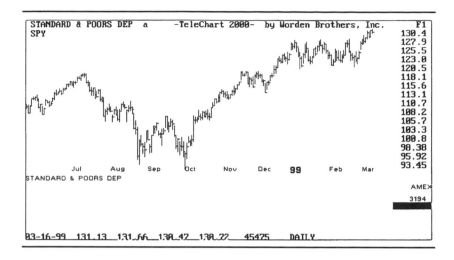

Look for dips. See how it has an upward bias.

MDY AND DIA

If you want a little more aggressive play you can invest the same way in the S&P 400, sometimes called the industrials. This is a second tier of great companies. The ticker is MDY. The trust is made up of the stock of the next level down of 400 companies, and it trades for one-tenth of the index.

If you like the Dow 30 or the DJIA, a trust has all 30 of these stocks. The ticker is DIA, it is called Diamonds. I guess that's DJIA without the "J."

I like SPY because it's a broader base, having 500 companies not just 30. SPY gives me a chance to own all of these 500 companies. I don't have to pick and choose, and I don't have to pay the high cost of mutual funds.

TAX INVESTING

There are many good REITS that really know their real estate stuff. Some throw off income. Some invest in undervalued properties. Those will do well if they're managed right.

At the time this book was written many REITS had backed off their high prices of a few years ago. Ironically, their Real Estate holdings have gone up in value. Many REITS are trading close to their Net Asset Value. There are many types of REITS available. Do your homework.

Other tax investing includes IRC Section 29 energy credits. A few companies produce income, with tax deductions (depletion allowance) and tax credits. That's right, actual credits, which offset, dollar for dollar, taxes owed. There are more, but check out Williams Coal Seam Royalty Trust (WTU), Burlington Resources (BRU) and Torch Energy (TRU). Study these out. Buy on dips. Buy to capture the dividend (four times a year) and you also get the tax credits.

EDUCATION

I'm dedicated to making our seminar company the best. Why, because my students demand it. Get in the educational mode. What is the value of one $10,000 idea used over and over again?

Stay a step ahead by knowing what your education can and will do for you.

One of the problems I see facing you is having to face your stockbrokers. Most of them are hardworking people. They get it. Others are myopic. They see so little. They understand less. You will spend a lot of time educating them. Some people, who have signed up for my workshops tell their stockbrokers they are attending the Wade Cook event. The brokers begin to bad-mouth me about my seminars.

They know not of what they speak. If they're not up on it, they're down on it. It is so easy to be critical and sarcastic. If they would just read my book or come to the events, they would say, "Wow, here is a down-to-earth, nuts and bolts event." "Here is pure education." "I want all of my clients to attend." Several brokers I know won't take on clients until they have taken our Wall Street Workshop™ course.

Please read the following comments from four brokers:

(Note: These four stockbrokers also came to work at Wade Cook Seminars, Inc. They are instructors of the Wall Street Workshop™ and other courses.)

"Brain washed is what I felt after a BS Degree in Finance and two years of stockbroker experience. You will learn more in the two-day Wall Street Workshop™ than you did with two years stockbroker experience, I would dare say 20 years of stockbroker experience.

Wade has put together cutting-edge, cash-producing, current strategies that can make a significant difference to anyone's brokerage account.

Don't fight it, join it!

Preston Christensen"

"As a former stockbroker, trained by the number one brokerage firm in the world, I approached the WSWS with great skepticism...primarily due to my experience during a very rigorous training regimen provided by my firm and the first one I worked for. Throughout both of these training programs (both over six months in length) not once was the issue of how to make money in the stock market even addressed.

I knew that there were long held, tried and true proven market formulas with which to provide my family with great wealth...however, I could not get anyone to teach them to me. It was as if it was some great "secret of the ages" that only a lucky few could be party to. With this in mind I attended my first Wall Street Workshop™ over two years ago. Lo and behold, not only did I find these formulas, but they were provided in a concise easy to understand (even for beginners) format that was "hands on."

I even got to do trades with instructors who had followed Wade's path before me. As a result, I have since attended every available teaching seminar offered by Wade Cook including five (count'em five) Wall Street Workshops™. Thanks to Wade Cook, my life, my family's lives, and future generation lives have changed as a result of these teachings. Thank God for Wade Cook!

Kurt Bolinder"

"As an active stockbroker, I did not take my first WSWS based solely on my own thirst for knowledge. It was only after persistent urging, and nagging, from my brother, a graduate of the WSWS, did I decide to finally attend. Actually, his actions spoke even louder than his words. He consistently made money in the stock market after he attended the WSWS. He even quit his job, making more money in the market using the short-term meter drop than I did using the long-term buy and hold. So I decided I might have some time to learn how the meter drop works.

When I came to the workshop I sat in the very last row, the seat closest to the door. I was hoping to escape at the first break if I found this was a waste of my time. Skeptical? No, not me. Well, my experience was a humbling one. I opened my mind, I realized I was very good at and knowledgeable about long-term investing and retirement planning, but I had never really looked at short-term investing such as the meter drop. I had never applied the strategies Wade simply teaches.

I now am eternally grateful to my brother for all the harassing phone calls he placed to me trying to convince me to attend the WSWS. And that I didn't have all the answers–that took some convincing. He also assured me my life will never be the same. After I reached the point I was making more money in the market than I did as a broker with over 800 clients, I quit my job.

I now have the satisfaction and peace of mind knowing that with the right knowledge and education I received by coming to all the classes offered by Wade that I will never have to work a day in my life again.

I've been blessed.

Stacy Acevedo"

"A year ago, I attended Wade Cook's Wall Street Workshop™. As a former stockbroker and an active trader, I was very skeptical that Wade Cook's workshop would enhance my trading skills. But guess what–I discovered that I was one of those stockbrokers that 'didn't get it.' Sure, I knew a lot about the stock market, but I was unaware of the numerous financial strategies that have literally changed my life. I now realized that I could do the very things taught at Wade's workshop for the rest of my life. Could I have gotten this same information as a stockbroker? I don't think so. Thank you Wade Cook.

Frank Leuck"

Those testimonials begin to tell the story. Your own success story is waiting to be written. Your story will have added depth if you diversify your strategies with different brokers. You see, one broker might really know covered calls; another knows options; another really "gets it" with spreads.

Also, if you have two or three different brokers you can usually reach one on the phone. They can help you discuss ideas. It is good for us to base our decisions on contrasting opinions. Just remember to whom are you listening? Be careful. Make sure they "get it."

Fun Forty-Nine

It is a sobering fact to consider how many individuals outpaced the big fund managers last year. However, conventional wisdom states that you should put your money into mutual funds. There are many people who are scared to invest on their own for a number of reasons:

- Stocks can be highly volatile.
- A person may feel they don't know enough to venture out on their own.
- With tech stocks, since 1980 only about 25% of the IPOs are trading above their offering price.
- Only a small percentage of stocks have experienced phenomenal success.

The main factor is that many people fear getting involved because they do not know enough about the various sectors. Here are some things you can do to help give you that "edge" to increase your chances of having profitable trades:

- Find the companies that are the leaders in their sector.
- Look at the company description; find out what it does.
- What is the market capitalization (value) of the company and how does it compare to others in the sector.
- What is its P/E (price to earnings) ratio and how does it compare to other companies in the sector?
- How much of it is institutionally held?

If you can do these things you can give yourself very valuable information about the companies you want to invest in. If you can do this, why not set up your own basket of stocks? If you set up your own group, then you can put stocks that you like in it. You do not have to follow any rules or instructions of a managing company like a fund manager has to do. And most important, you have the freedom to change the stocks in your basket at your discretion. By doing this you can greatly diversify your portfolio. I admit, you won't get the kind of gains that you would if you were buying, say, an Internet stock, but then you won't have all of your eggs in one basket, and you'll be able to sleep well.

After you get your basket together, compare how it is doing against top funds. If it is not doing as well or much better, you might want to consider changing the percentage allocation, or even changing which stocks make up the basket.

One of the problems with mutuals, especially in the tech sector, is that you can find fund managers that get into tech stocks just for the sake of being in them. These usually don't give you the kind of returns you could achieve if you were to do your homework and put together your own selections. A lot of funds have set entry and exit points, which is excellent, but if a company has some good news and a big run up, whereas the mutual has a set exit point, you can easily cancel your sell order and adjust it accordingly. And when it comes to setting your exit points this should be treated with as much, if not more emphasis than your entry point. Make sure you are getting out for the right reasons. Be it bad news that could have a long-term effect; fundamentals that have gone sour, or over-valuation of the stock. Please do not let emotion get the better of you, and cause you to bail out on a little down draft. Pay attention to the charts. Check support levels.

What you would like to do is to be into the companies that lead their sectors. And since these are leaders, this could end up being a costly process. Here are some things you can do to help offset the cost of purchasing these stocks:

- Consider buying the stocks on margin.
- Do these in a discount or deep discount account.

- Buy on downdrafts or dips.
- Sell puts to buy the stocks at a discount.
- Write calls on the stocks to generate income and lower your cost basis.

When you put together your own basket, you will in effect be setting up your own mutual fund–just on a much smaller scale. To that end, this will not be a simple task. You won't just be able to throw darts to make your choices. Do your homework–look at what the fund managers do and try to emulate what they do. Admittedly, the fund mangers have millions of dollars for research. You probably don't have these kind of dollars at your disposal, but you can still look at Wealth Information Network™ (W.I.N.™), get into Research, and look at company fundamentals and earnings. Find a web site or publication that profiles the CEO. Look at earnings: past, present, and future.

To whom are you listening? Look and listen to what the big boys do, then put in perspective for your own situation and reap the benefits. The following page is a list we have come up with that we call our Fun(damental) Forty-Nine. We've picked seven major sectors and listed the leaders in them. Your choices may vary, but this could be a good starting point for doing your own research.

FUN(DAMENTAL) FORTY-NINE

TECHS	RETAILS
1. Microsoft (MSFT)	1. Wal-Mart (WMT)
2. Intel (INTC)	2. Home Depot (HD)
3. International Business Machines (IBM)	3. Gap Stores (GPS)
4. Cisco Systems (CSCO)	4. Dayton Hudson (HD)
5. Dell (DELL)	5. Safeway (SWY)
6. Oracle (ORCL)	6. Lowe's Companies (LOW)
7. America Online (AOL)	7. Costco (COST)

CONGLOMERATE	OIL
1. General Electric (GE)	1. Mobil (MOB)
2. Proctor & Gamble (PG)	2. BP Amoco PLC-Spons Adr (BPA)
3. Slumberger (SLB)	3. Chevron (CHV)
4. United Technologies (UTX)	4. Exxon (XON)
5. Colgate-Palmolive (CL)	5. Arco (ARC)
6. Clorox (CLX)	6. Texaco (TX)
7. Phillip Morris (MO)	7. Royal Dutch [a.k.a. Shell] (RD)

BANKS	MANUFACTURING
1. Citigroup (C)	1. Ford (F)
2. Bankamerica Corp (BAC)	2. General Motors (GM)
3. J. P. Morgan (JPM)	3. Union Carbide (UK)
4. Chase Manhattan Bank (CMB)	4. Boeing Co (BA)
5. Bank One Corp (ONE)	5. Minnesota Mining and Manufacturing (MMM)
6. Mellon Bank (MEL)	6. Allied Signal (ALD)
7. Wells Fargo (WFC)	7. Caterpillar (CAT)

OTHER

1. Merck (MRK)
2. Pfizer (PFE)
3. United Airlines (UAL)
4. American Airlines (AMR)
5. Lucent (LU)
6. AT & T (T)
7. American International Group (AIG)

A good character is, in all cases,
the fruit of personal exertion.
It is not inherited from parents;
it is not created by external
advantages; it is no necessary
appendage of birth, wealth,
endeavors—the fruit and reward of
good principles manifested in a course
of virtuous and honorable action.

Joel Hawes

CHAPTER 6

COMPANY NEWS AND QUARTERLY EARNINGS

Recently, I've noticed a relationship between quarterly SEC filings, news reports, "whisper" number, and the like. I asked our trading department to start a research project on this phenomenon. While our research is not complete, as of the printing of this book I felt it still important to disseminate this news as fast as possible. This is a very important. See wadecook.com for continual updates.

"Microsoft-conference-call..." The sheer terror those three words can inspire rivals just about any fear in the world of stock market trading, especially if you have a hi-tech position. That's why I shuddered when I read a Bloomberg news bulletin a few days ago that Microsoft had called a conference call for after the market close. I worried that, after all of the tech purging of the last few weeks, my investments in Dell Computer (DELL) were about to take another serious hit. What happens if Microsoft confirms that PC sales are slowing, I thought to myself? What happens if they admit that some computer companies have too much inventory or that others "stuffed the channel" with merchandise to get it off their books? These thoughts bounced through my head as I watched DELL, which has no inventory problems itself, drop like a stone after the Bloomberg signal. Company news can help or hurt your trade, so you have to pay attention to it. Fortunately, news follows a pattern that you can learn about, and which may just give you another handle to control a trade. Please read on, because the powerful insights described below will not only help you stay out of trouble, it may even help improve your market timing.

Our boss, Wade Cook, is a savvy Wall Street trader. Years of investing have given him the insight that as a company's quarterly reporting period approaches, news about the company increases, and this dynamic may cause upward pressure on the stock price. In Wade's pattern, a company initiates two to four week price trend by generating published reports and holding news conferences leading to the posting of its quarterly earnings report. Wall Street experts, called analysts, present their neutral views. These specialists analyze the company's data and publish their own views on how the company is doing. Their comments include expectations which a company must meet to show that it is on target, and this is how a company justifies the price valuation of its stock. When the company misses the analysts' "number," the price of its stock often corrects to a lower level. As this high-profile, "newsy" activity increases and corresponding to whether the news is positive or negative, the price of the stock will tend up or down leading to the posting of the quarterly earnings report. Having made these observations, Wade asked the Research and Trading Department at Wade Cook Financial to study this market phenomenon. The following paragraphs illustrate Wade's observations about company news and quarterly earnings, which the department was able to confirm and detail. Dell Computer Corporation (DELL) will serve to model the pattern.

DELL's last quarterly period ended January 31, 1999. Earnings were posted on February 16th. As the quarterly period drew to a close, the volume of positive "newsy" items increased and the stock rose to a new high at $110 a share. Market sentiment anticipated a positive earnings report and a possible stock split announcement. DELL also rose on the rumor that it was about to launch an expansive Internet venture to increase online sales. After January 31, DELL drew back in price as if to catch it's breath and consolidate for a move up on the announcements. On February 10th, Wade Cook entered the public trading area at the Semper Financial Conference in Los Angeles where the Research and Trading Department was projecting a Bloomberg, real-time, options chain of Dell Computer Corporation onto a large screen

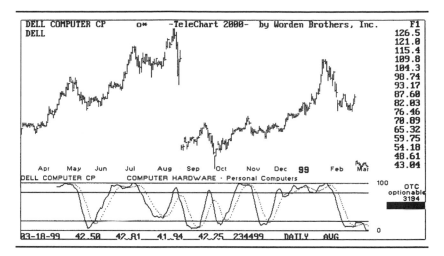

in the front of the room. Wade assessed the trend and placed a trade on DELL with his broker. Within 20 minutes, Wade had made about $10,000 and had closed the trade with a second phone call without leaving the room. Wade was very impressive that morning. Unfortunately, I chose to hold onto my DELL options, feeling confident that "invincible" DELL would meet the analysts' expectations and make more impressive gains. The next day, February 11th, DELL continued its upward trend, and I caught a flight home from the conference feeling assured the trade would work out. The next morning, my broker phoned me to report that the trade had been stopped out at a loss. Almost in disbelief I asked why, and learned that two analysts from large brokerage firms had published concerns that DELL may slip in its percentage of revenue growth. The stock fell six points at the opening on February 12th, and another six points throughout the trading day. The market was closed February 15th for the President's holiday. On February 16th, DELL rebounded recovering half the points it lost on the analysts' pre-announcement warning. After the market closed on February 16th, DELL posted earnings that actually beat the analysts' expectations. The company also announced a 2:1 stock split, but, as predicted, DELL missed a beat and posted slower annual revenue growth, a drop from 55 to 38%. In spite of all the other positive news and announcements, the bad news regarding revenue growth slowing was enough to torpedo Dell and cause the price to sink lower.

Dell Computer Corporation is heavily traded and many investors lost money during this period. If they had known about Wade's quarterly-earnings, company-news pattern, however, they might have been able to take profits instead of losses. Let me explain why. Analyzing the quarterly-earnings pattern, the first thing you should notice is that the increase in newsy items prior to a company's quarterly earnings often produces a predictable up-trend prior to the posting date. So, if an investor knew when a company's quarterly period ended, he or she could take a position in the market intended and profit from the predictable uptrend. The last few days prior to the announcement itself, however, are dangerous, because that is the time analysts may issue warnings about the company, and their comments may cause the price to gap lower. With the announcement date still a few days away, an investor could lock in his or her profits from the uptrend by closing out early. That's what Wade did at the Semper Financial Conference in Los Angeles. He correctly assessed that DELL was in a significant uptrend, placed a short-term trade, and got out three days before the posting. He correctly anticipated that the days just before DELL's earnings announcement would be highly volatile and could cut both ways.

Summarizing, an investor should do his or her homework and know when a company's quarterly periods end, the day the company is likely to post earnings, and what the analysts' are saying before an earnings announcement. He or she can't obtain the actual content of the report prior to the posting. That would be "insider information," which is regulated by the Securities and Exchange Commission. If it were allowed, "insider information" would give some traders an unfair advantage at the expense of others. So, the SEC requires companies to guard the contents of an earning's report with tight security. Without knowing the actual contents, an investor is betting on the possibilities, and hoping he or she has guessed the right way. Knowing these dates would enable the investor to enter the market four to six weeks ahead of the earnings report, take advantage of the predictable uptrend, and then sell the position one to three days before the actual announcement.

Dow Jones Industrials

Wade's quarterly-earnings, company-news pattern functions more like a guideline than a rule. The difference is that guidelines apply to high probability outcomes and may be broken from time to time as outside elements interfere with the pattern. Rules, on the other hand, may not be broken without invalidating a principle. Examples from the Dow Jones Industrial 30 show how this works.

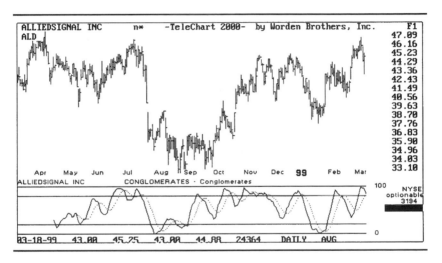

Allied Signal Inc. (ALD) closes its fiscal year on December 31st. The company last reported earnings on January 20, 1999. The analysts' expected an earnings posting of .617¢ a share. ALD reported .630¢ a share beating the estimates by 2.11%. Earnings rose 14% during the fourth quarter of 1998. One would expect a perfect correlation to the guideline with this example. It correlated, but not perfectly. About four weeks before the posting, ALD began a strong uptrend which ended prematurely during the first week in January, due largely to aviation industry sector problems that pulled ALD lower in sympathy. After the positive earnings posting on January 20, and a period of consolidation lasting about a week, the stock moved higher on strength.

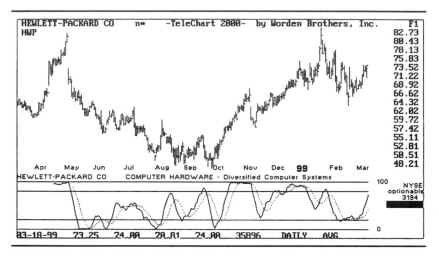

Hewlett-Packard Company (HWP) closes its fiscal books on
October 31st. The company reported earnings on November 16,
1998, and then again on February 16, 1999. The analysts' expected earnings of .748¢ a share in November and .826¢ a share in
February. HWP reported .690¢ a share disappointing the estimates by 7.75%. About six weeks before the posting, HWP began
a surging uptrend which lasted until the earnings were reported
on November 16. After the disappointing report, HWP dropped
sharply. Four weeks prior to the posting in February, HWP
moved forward again anticipating the earnings report. The stock
went to a new high, consolidated back, and surged forward until
February 16th. This time HWP reported .950¢ a share earnings
beating expectations by 15.01%.

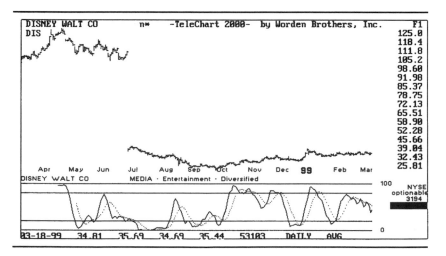

The Walt Disney Company (DIS) closes its fiscal year on September 30th. The company reported earnings on November 3, 1998, and then again on January 27, 1999. The analysts' expected earnings of .152¢ a share in November and .239¢ a share in February. DIS reported .140¢ a share disappointing estimates by 7.89%. About four weeks before the posting, DIS began a surging uptrend which stalled on November 3rd. After the disappointing report, DIS traded sideways. Four weeks prior to the posting in January, DIS moved forward again, even gapping to a new high, anticipating the earnings report. This time DIS reported .300¢ a share earnings beating expectations by 25.52%. Even after this outstanding report, the stock consolidated and has been trading sideways since January 27th.

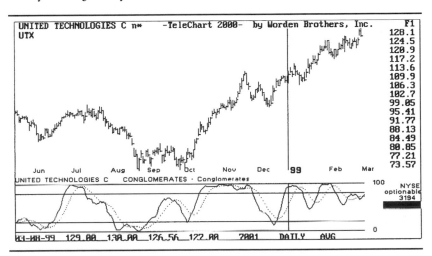

United Technologies Corporation (UTX) closes its fiscal books on December 31st. The company reported earnings on January 21, 1999. The analysts' expected earnings of $1.105 a share. UTX reported $1.23 a share beating the estimates by 11.31%. About four weeks before the posting, HWP began a surging uptrend which lasted until the earnings were reported. Since the posting, the company has continued to surge forward.

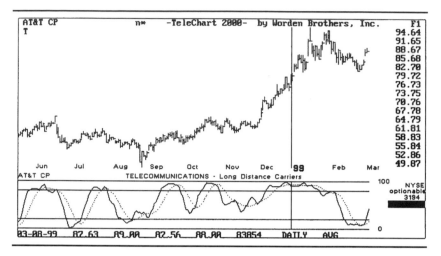

AT&T Corporation (T) closes its fiscal books on December 31st. The company reported earnings on January 25, 1999. The analysts' expected earnings of $1.002 a share. AT&T reported $1.140 a share beating the estimates by 13.77%. About six weeks before the posting, HWP began a surging uptrend which lasted until the earnings were reported. After the positive report, AT&T continued uptrending for about one week and then dropped off consolidating.

CHAPTER 7

DIVERSIFY FORMULAS

In our never-ending quest to make as much profits as possible, we must turn once again to the area of loss avoidance. While there is no way to avoid losses entirely (except with the sell put, buyback and roll out formula) there certainly are ways to avoid making common mistakes and halting the stupid things we do to lose money or, at least not make so much money as we can on a particular trade.

This chapter will primarily deal with options. Some of these same concepts also apply to stock and mutual fund investing.

DIVERSIFICATION

I've written on diversification elsewhere. Those sections cover the "why tos and how tos." Typically you will hear ideas about a need to own different types of stock, and occasionally these categories are broken down into stocks for income, stocks for growth, or a blend of stocks. Mutual fund investing is designed to be diversification epitomized. This diversification process is good in an unusual way, as the search makes people think about their own needs, now and in the future. Hopefully they will start to do their own research into the investments needed to fulfill their needs.

Along comes Wade Cook and says not only is this form of diversification important, but that you also need to learn and diversify your formulas or methods of making money. There are specific strategies for capturing profits. You need a diversity of formulas, not just your stocks.

About these strategies:

1. Some have more risk. Some are really safe.

2. Some are easier than others to implement. Some take study and practice.

3. Some you can use in tandem. Some are single use.

4. All have a specific place to be used.

Precision is so important. Each tool has a use. We need to study the market and a stock's movements to know which one to use.

I'm reminded of "Turkey Man." He took about $15,000 and had it over $560,000 in just over a year. That is phenomenal. Most of my students don't achieve this kind of success. He bought a condo in Hawaii, then shortly thereafter he wanted a job in our sales department! I questioned why. He had made so much money. "But now it's gone," he said. How? "Well, I put all of it in two options out the next month–and they went down." "Where did you ever learn this?" I questioned. He felt bad. Here's the lesson. Don't bet it all on "red." Don't get cocky. Don't think that you're invincible. Stay in the game. Don't ever do anything that causes you to quit.

If you're an athlete, don't do that which would cause you to quit. You would never go to Las Vegas and put all of your money on one number. In fact, the Las Vegas comparison can be used more. But first a quick question: Did you hear about the guy who went to Vegas in his $40,000 Cadillac and came home in a $400,000 bus?

Most of us know that if we go to a gambling place and leave all the money on the table, the house will eventually take it back. That is the design. You can't stay exposed with all of your money. It may take hours or days–but you will give it back. A song by Kenny Rogers comes to mind. Let's walk away with our profits. My friend Turkey Man should have done several small plays. He knew this. That is our training. Meter Drop–get in, get out, make money.

A $2,000 Kind Of Guy

Let's say you decide that $10,000 is your "active money" amount, your risk money, or at least the money that you'll use for aggressive trading. Do you put it all on one play, or several?

I say you do five smaller trades of around $2,000 each. Even if that means that you do three contracts of one option and seven contracts of another. Now, you'll hardly ever do exactly $2,000, but one will be $1,900, the next one $2,150. It's close enough.

Another way would be to figure it by a percentage. Say, 10% or 20% of your fun money will go into one particular strategy. Your principal shifts all the time, so I stay with a dollar amount for ease of thinking. And stay with this amount for a long time. Stay with it until you conscientiously and (when the market is closed) make a decision to move up to $3,000 trades or $5,000 trades. Don't make this decision in the heat of battle.

You see, you may build up your $10,000 to $40,000 and then want to do $4,000 trades. Why would you quit doing that which is successful? ($40,000 in 20 trades of $2,000 are my way to go.) Don't get big-deal-itis. Have you ever seen a football team get the ball on their own two yard line, then pop, bam, all the way down the field? One pass after another. They're on the opponent's three yard line and three times they try to run it in—then end up missing a field goal—and losing the game. Don't quit doing successful things.

I know it's tempting, but remember precision and discipline. Learn from your small trades. Earn while you learn. Learn to apply what you've learned in small trades to other small trades. Don't think that now that you've made $3,000 on a $2,000 trade that $20,000 will make $30,000. Stick with eating the whole supper, but one bite at a time.

Let me share with you a common situation. One has $10,000 to invest in options.

Trade	A	=	$1,000	is a call option on a dip.
	B	=	$1,000	is an option on a stock split.
	C	=	$2,000	is a sell put trade.

Then you hear about another stock split on a great company and you put in the balance or $6,000.

$$D = \$6,000.$$

Trade A breaks even–you just keep your $1,000. You lose on trade B and kiss goodbye $1,000. Trade C makes you $500 and you get a nice 10% return on trade D, or $600. You're right or almost right on three trades out of four.

You've made $1,100 and lost $1,000. After commissions you're probably underwater a little. It's sad. You've gone the whole month to make nothing.

Now, let's start over. Take the $10,000 and do five $2,000 trades, or ten $1,000 trades. Now, if you're right a majority of the time, say three out of five; or seven out of ten, you'll make steady money.

It's very common to see the profits on big trades wiped out by a few small losers. Stick with even trade amounts.

ENEMY TERRITORY

Let me use a military example. You're close to enemy territory; you spot an enemy site.

SAFE TERRITORY	ENEMY TERRITORY
O = You	X = Target

Would you take a whole battalion in or would you send in a small squad of say eight men? Obviously you want to scout it out and wipe out the post if you can; if it doesn't endanger the bigger operation. Let's go in with our $2,000 squad.

SAFE TERRITORY	ENEMY TERRITORY
O	X^1
$2,000 ➤	$2,000
	Plus $1,500 profits captured
	$3,500 total

Now you spot X^2. Should you go get it with your $3,500? No, that's not the mission. Get back to safe territory. Don't stay behind enemy lines.

SAFE TERRITORY	ENEMY TERRITORY
	X^2
$3,500 ◄——————◄	$3,500

Now from a position of strength and after getting cool, calm and collected, make another decision.

A) SAFE TERRITORY	ENEMY TERRITORY
O = $2,000 ➡➡ Look for target	
	X^3

Take the $1,500 off
to blue chip investments
or pay some bills.

Or, if you really don't need the money divide the $3,500 ($2,000 + $1,500) into two plays.

B) SAFE TERRITORY	ENEMY TERRITORY
O = $1,700 ➡———➡	X^3
	$1,000 capture
O = $1,700 ◄———————◄	X^4
	$3,000 capture, wow!

Now get all the money back to safe territory and repeat the process. Soon you will have $10,000, then maybe $20,000 and some-day $100,000, but it will get captured if you leave it all at risk. Do whatever you can to thwart the house from getting back your chips.

BALANCING PORTFOLIO STRATEGIES

Once you've proportioned your portfolio to accommodate each strategy you will have to make a decision as to when to trade.

Example Portfolio (Aggressive/Semi-passive part)

20%	Rolling Stocks
40%	Covered Calls
20%	Options
10%	Bargain Stocks
10%	Spreads

In a downtrending market you may not be doing a bunch of "buy call" strategies, covered calls, or bull put spreads.

The point here is just because you have established percentages of your portfolio to different types of strategies, don't feel obligated to trade every strategy and/or trade with all of your money all of the time. Realize that the only money you should be trading with is the money allocated to the strategy that will work for the current market environment. Once a market changes, go back to paper trading until you figure it out and get profitable consistently.

EVEN INCREMENTS—VARIOUS FORMULAS

Another by-product of even trades, and using diversified formulas is that your profit will be steadier. One loss on a bigger trade won't wipe out the profits on many smaller trades.

Another advantage of having different strategies available is that you will have different weapons to use in various situations. If XYZ stock is on a serious dip, we can:

1. Buy stock.
    a. Own and then sell.
    b. Own and write covered calls later.
2. Buy call options.
3. Sell puts.

4. Do bull put spreads.

5. Do bull call spreads.

If XYZ is a roller, we can:

1. Buy stock when low, and then put in sell order.

2. Buy calls at bottom, buy puts at top.

3. Do rolling options.

4. Do bull put spreads and bull call spreads when low.

5. Do bear call spreads and bear put spreads when high.

6. Sell naked calls, sell puts.

If stock has peaked up, then we can:

1. Buy puts.

2. Do bear call spreads and bear put spreads.

3. Sell calls.

4. Unload stock.

Which weapon? Well, in the army you are trained on various weapons. Some people go on to become specialists in a particular weapon. Which one? It depends on your training and expertise. It depends on your risk tolerance. It depends on which one is fun for you.

Practice, Diversify, Practice

A man may be outwardly successful all his life long, and die hollow and worthless as a puffball; and he may be externally defeated all his life long, and dies in the royalty of a kingdom established within him—A man's true estate of power and riches, is to be in himself; not in his dwelling, or position, or external relations, but in his own essential character.—That is the realm in which he is to live, if he is to live as a Christian man.

Henry Ward Beecher

CHAPTER 8

WRITING "IN-THE-MONEY" CALLS

Writing covered calls is a workhorse formula. Writing calls produces cash flow each month and turns traditional stock holdings into "rental stocks." To add safety to this strategy we will do the deals in the money. Writing in-the-money calls takes away the downside loss potential, not completely, but almost completely–if we do this strategy correctly by following the formula. A discussion of writing covered calls is necessary before we add on the "in-the-money" fine tuning part of this cash flow method. Simply put, writing means selling. A call is a call option, and covered in this strategy means we own the underlying stock. So, all together we are selling an option, thereby generating income against the stocks we own. The premium income is in our account in one day. We agree to sell the stock at a set price. We have to keep the stock (and remain covered) until one of the following occurs.

1. The expiration date is reached and we are either called out (the stock is bought away from us) or not called out (we keep the stock).

2. We get called out early–before the expiration date. This would be nice, although it happens infrequently, as we would accelerate our profits to that point.

3. We end the position by buying back the call–hopefully at less than what we sold it for, so we get a net profit on just the option play.

Here's an example:

We do covered calls by buying the stock on dips, and to double up our profits we can purchase the stock on margin by putting up half the money.

XYZ Company's stock is on a dip down to $17. When it starts back up we buy the stock for $18. It has a previous high of $27. The next month out (March) $20 calls are going for $1. When the stock hits $19.25 the calls are $1.50. We sell them and take in the $1.50. Ten contracts would be $1,500. We bought 1,000 shares (you can do 100, 700, 1,200, or whatever, but do the stock purchase in 100 share increments or groups as option contracts are for 100 shares). Now, what have we done? By selling an option we have taken on an obligation to sell or deliver the stock at the $20 price! That would be nice, because we purchased the stock for $18. (And, 1,000 shares at this additional $2 profit would be another $2,000.)

We also get to keep the $1,500 either way. That's a $3,500 profit on a $9,000 investment, ($18,000 divided by 2 for margin = $9,000). If the stock does not go above $20, say only to $19.50 or so, we keep the $1,500 plus we still have the stock. Now after the third Friday of March, we can sell the April $20 calls for $2 and take in another $2,000. Is this fun or what?

IN YOUR PORTFOLIO

Do you own stocks? Okay, try it on paper. Let's say you own General Motors at $58. You purchased it for $40 and you own 300 shares. The $60 calls for next month are going for $3. That's $3 times 300 shares or $900, or $1 for the higher strike price of $65, or $300. Which one? The question is do you want to get called out or not. If you think the stock might go up above $60 and you want to get called out then sell the $60 calls. If you don't want to lose the stock sell the $65 calls. It's likely that the stock will go above $65 eventually–but not by the third Friday of the next month. It's up to you. One way to generate more cash is selling the $60 calls, but there is a higher potential of getting called out. The other way (sell-ing the $65 calls) produces less cash, but you'll sell at a higher price.

CALLED OUT

Do you have to do anything if you get called out? No. It all hap-pens electronically. If the stock is above $60, on Monday after the third Friday, your broker will tell you that you were called out. Your confirmation slip will say "account assigned" and three days later (Thursday, if there are no holidays) the $18,000 ($60 X 300 shares) will be in your account.

Exercising options is a random thing. If your stock is at 59^{7}\!/_{8}$ or 60^{1}\!/_{8}$ you may or may not get called out. If the stock is at 60^{1}\!/_{2}$ you will get called out.

GET BACK IN CONTROL

When you write a call you are giving up the upside potential of the stock. If our $18 stock is a flyer, say new ratings or target esti-mates of $30 are out, then you shouldn't be writing a call at $20. By doing so you've agreed to sell the stock at $20. If you have stocks you want to keep don't write calls on them. Or write calls so far out of the money–say a $25 strike price in our example (even if for 25¢, or $250) that it is unlikely you will get called out.

Now, here's a way to get back the stock, and in fact regain the upside potential. The stock spikes up to $21, quickly, the $20 call is now $2.75 you sold it for $1.50, or $1,500. You now buy the same call for $2.75 or $2,750. You're now at a loss of $1,250, but you own the stock with no option positions written against it. If it moves up to $24 or $27 you could just keep it, sell it or write the $25 calls or the $30 calls against it.

This process is called a "buy back." We sold it. Now we buy it back. A roll out is where we move out and sell the next month's option for a higher price or sell this month's option at a higher strike price. Look at two scenarios.

1. The stock is at $21. The March $20 call is $2.75 but the April $20 call is $4.25. Buy back the March position. We're down the $1,250 but sell the April options and take in

81

$4,250. We're now up $3,000, plus we'll probably make the $2,000 for buying the stock at $18 and selling it for $20. We could buy it back in April and do this all over again.

2. The stock is at $21, but the time value of the premium erodes as we get close to the March expiration date. The option price comes down to say $1.25 or $1,250. If we buy the same options now we're still profitable by $250 ($1,500 original sale price with $250 cost of buying back the same options). Now, see "A" and roll it out (and/or up) to the April date.

Cash flow and control—what else do you want?

What If The Stock Goes Down?

Oops! The stock doesn't perform the way it should. This happens, but not too frequently, if you really do your homework. We do this strategy on dips—and not right when it goes down, we wait for the stock to start back up.

We also check...

1. Market indications. It's hard for a stock to break the trend.

2. Sector evaluation. How are other stocks doing in the same industry or sector?

3. Fundamentals. How is it doing? Is it earning money? Check the other fundamental measuring sticks that are important to you.

4. News. Is there controversy, or good news? Has the good news played out? Will it take awhile before it heads back up and gets close to or above the next strike price?

5. Options shop for a good price. Put in your order to sell the call when the stock rises.

6. Be aware of the latest developments. Are there buy ratings on the stock, et cetera?

Now, you're ready. If you're not confident of making a profit—stay out. This is not a gamble but close to a sure deal. Your research will make it that way. Practice on paper until you get good at this.

However, with all this in mind and after doing our homework, the stock dips after you buy it. You have also sold the calls. Obviously you won't get called out. The stock is below the strike price. Now that the stock is down, you have more opportunities.

An $18 stock goes to $19, then crashes to $16. You get off the call for $1 at the $20 strike price. Our cost basis in the stock is now $17 ($18 minus the $1 of premium income). A week later it's at $15. Now what do you do?

Obviously you won't get called out at $20 unless it runs back up quickly, so you could...

1. Just let it ride until the expiration date. (I'm usually not in favor of this.)

2. You could buy back the option for, say 25¢. The cost is $250 and your net for selling the original option is $750. You spend $250 to end (close) the position. Now that we have the stock freed up we can...

   a. Wait it out.

   b. Sell it at a loss (not me, usually).

   c. Sell the $15 or the $17.50 call to generate more income.

   d. Go to the next month and sell the $15 or $17.50 call.

If the stock has bottomed out, start selling calls as it moves back up. Sometimes the position becomes hopeless and we just have to weed the garden—get out of losing positions and re-deploy our money elsewhere.

SELLING IN-THE-MONEY CALLS

Because this is distasteful let's see if we can fine-tune this strategy. To make this work on all eight cylinders consider this: we buy the stock at $18 and sell the $17.50 calls for say $2. The stock is 50¢ in the money, $18 is 50¢ above the strike price of $17.50. If you take in $2 or $2,000 and the stock moves up you will get called out if you do nothing. You would have to give back 50¢ and your net profit would be $1,500. What is "give back?" It's jargon for "lose." You buy the stock for $18,000 and sell it for $17,500—do you see the $500 loss? Take that against our $2,000 income and we have $1,500.

Why do this? Because we want to get called out. We don't want to end up with a bunch of dogs in our account. Let's keep going. You've also done your homework. You've caught this stock on a dip, you wait for a bounce or a few upticks, and now sell the $17.50 call for $3 or so. That's $3,000 of income.

What if it drops now? Do you see that the stock would have to drop to $15 before you lose money? (Note: $18,000 minus the $3,000 premium income means you have an adjusted basis of $15,000.) You're still profitable down to $15, below $15 and you start losing money.

Now what if it goes up? Once again you can just let the stock be taken away from you or buy back the option. Let's say the stock moves to $20 or $21. You could buy back the $17.50 call and sell the $20 or the $22.50 calls. The opportunities are not unlimited, but almost. At least we have a way to get in control and make money.

Selling in-the-money calls is a small insurance policy. If the stock falls a little, we're still long at the current strike price. If it falls a lot, our loss is lessened because we have the bigger premium for selling an in-the-money call. The main point is that we have our original cash back in, plus the option premium.

Note: We do bull call spreads slightly in the money for much of the same reason.

Report from Research and Trading

Wade did an interesting trade this morning on CMGI Inc. (CMGI) that may need some explanation. The stock was trading this morning around $192. The company has been moving strongly upwards the last couple of days. There is news today. CMGI owns a 20% share stake in Lycos (LCOS), the CMGI Inc. Chief Executive Officer (CEO) does not like the merger proposal that USA Networks (USAI) has offered for Lycos (LCOS). He resigned from the Lycos Board of Directors today as part of CMGI's strategy to keep USA Networks (USAI) from buying Lycos or at least having them re-negotiate for a better deal. He resigned because he is now free to lobby on behalf of CMGI without having any responsibility to Lycos. Along with the news on the stock, they also are a potential stock split candidate. The company will report their earnings on Thursday, so there is the possibility of a split announcement at that time. The last time they announced a split, the stock was around $90, well below the current price. Wade bought 200 shares at $192. This was purchased on margin; meaning that half of the money needed to buy the stock comes in the form of a loan from your broker. Buying 200 shares at $192 costs $38,400. If you divide that in half, you have to put up $19,200 to buy the stock, the other $19,200 being a margin loan from your broker. Then Wade sold a call against the stock. He sold two contracts of the January 2000, $160 calls for $83. That brings into the account $16,600 ($83 multiplied by 200). The interesting thing about this play is, when you sell a call on the stock, the call premium brought in counts against your margin requirement. In other words, you have purchased the stock with 50% of the money on margin, but you can use the cash coming into your account from the calls to offset the cash that you have to bring in for the trade. Wade had to put up $96 in cash (or a total of $19,200), minus the $83 premium brought in (or $16,600), which means that you actually only have to come up with $13 per share for the trade. Take the 200 shares times the $13 and you actually only have to put up $2,600 in cash to get into this trade.

Basically you are into the stock at $13, plus a loan of $96, and you have written a covered call with a strike price of $160. To figure out your break-even point, or the lowest price the stock needs to be at for you to not lose anything on the trade, you add the amount that you have borrowed on margin ($96) and the amount of cash you had to put up for the trade ($13). This equals $109 per share. All the stock has to do is be somewhere between $109 and $160 in order to profit on this particular trade. Ideally, if you get called out at $160, you get the full upside of the stock and the law of leverage works here because you are only into it for $13. If the stock ends up below $109, you have lowered your downside by selling the call option when you bought the stock.

You need to check with your broker's margin requirements, as they are different from firm to firm. For example, some firms have recently increased the margin requirements on volatile Internet stocks (such as CMGI). Instead of having a minimum requirement of 30% margin, they have been increased to 50%. This means that you would generate a margin call (meaning you would have to put additional money in your account) if the stock closed below the price you purchased the stock at, assuming that you purchased it on 50% margin. If you have a broker that only requires 30% margin, you have a cushion below the price you purchased the stock at before a margin call would be generated. In our CMGI trade, the stock would have to close below about $155 for a margin call to be generated. Although your broker's margin department has complicated formulas to figure all of this out, generally you get a margin call when the stock price drops by about 20%.

This is the type of trade we put on W.I.N.™ all the time. W.I.N.™ is a great resource wherein real I post trades for my subscribers to read. It's great tutorial information because you can look over the shoulder of people who trade and make money in the stock market every day. You'll see trades not only from me, but also from my Team Wall Street instructors.

If you call now and mention this book, I'll make you a special introductory offer–five days of W.I.N.™ for only $10. That's five days full of trades, plus access to our great research sections and the journal of trades, which shows you what we've been doing for the last few months. Don't miss out. Call 1-800-872-7411 today.

TWO OUT OF THREE CHANCES FOR MAKING MONEY

I've repeatedly taught this in my workshops. When we sell options we have a two in three chance of making money. When we buy an option we have a one in three chance. Look at the same numbers. If the stock is $18 and it goes up and we own the $17.50 call, having bought it for say $1.50 or $1,500 for 10 contracts, we make money. If the stock goes down we lose, if it stays the same we lose. The only way to win is if the stock goes up.

Now let's be a seller, not a buyer. We sell the $17.50 for the same $1,500. If the stock goes up we win. If the stock stays the same we win. That's two out of three. But wait, there's more. If the stock goes down a little we can still make some money as the premium lessens our losses. We can perhaps still make money say if the stock dips from \$18 to \$16.50 or \$17. Now, this third way—adjusting the basis potentially gives up a three in three chance of making money. If you're serious about making money, I think you'll also learn that selling options is the way to go.

Practice, Sell, Practice

All that I have accomplished,
or expect or hope to accomplish,
has been and will be by that plodding,
patient, perservering process of
accretion which builds the ant-heap,
particle by particle, thought by
thought, fact by fact.

Elihu Burritt

CHAPTER 9

SELLING NAKED CALLS
AND BULL CALL SPREADS

$\mathbb{A}$ good starting place to understand and use bull call spreads would be a discussion of writing calls and comparing covered vs. uncovered calls. I've written extensively on covered calls, but what about writing an uncovered call? What are the added risks and profits? What is gained and lost?

Writing an uncovered call is different than writing a covered call in the simple fact that you do not own the stock. Ponder this!

You agree to sell stock that you don't own. For example, a stock has run up from $42 to $48, the $50 call is going for $3. You sell it. Once again for this chapter we'll use 10 contracts for our examples. Three dollars times 10 contracts, or $3 times 1,000 shares is $3,000. We receive $3,000 and we've taken on the obligation to sell the stock at $50. But we don't own the stock. Should we be worried? Yes.

We really start worrying as the stock goes above $50. In this case, we don't think it will. We've studied it out, $48 is a high for the stock, and we think the price will back off. If the stock stays below $50 by the expiration date, the option (and hence the obligation) expires and we get to keep the $3,000. Owari, end, fini, over and out.

A quick note about short-term plays and long-term plays. In all my examples we sell the options the next month out—even if it's three weeks or three days. When we buy calls or stock, usually we want to own the position for as long as we can afford to. However when we sell, we want to reduce the obligation time, the commitment to perform, to as short a time as possible. In short:

Buying = Long term
Selling = Short term

Our responsibility to profits is to be careful and make the most cash with the least risk as possible. That means we do these plays on good stocks, know the stock's movement, and buy the appropriate option—one where we will get the biggest bang for the buck.

BUY BACK AND KEEP THE PROFITS

Another play would be to sell the option for $3 and if and when the stock pulls back to $46 or $44, and the option drops to say $1, buy it back. Spend the $1,000 and close out the position. In this case, you keep the $2,000 Less Transaction Cost (LTC). This play is a lot of fun and quickly profitable. The reason pullbacks are profitable on sold positions is that they happen fast. The stock spikes up. Many people start to sell (profit taking) and the stock drops back a few dollars. We don't need the stock to drop to $42 again. A $3 or $4 drop could easily have $2 fall out of the $50 call option.

If you want more safety, sell the $55 call, for say $1. Generate $1,000 of income and move your commitment up a whole $5 strike price. Then, once again, let it expire or buy it on a pull back.

MARGIN—WHAT WILL IT BE?

The margin, or hold requirement in your account depends on the brokerage firm. Thirty percent is probably about where most will be. Thirty percent of what? In this case, your commitment amount is about $15,000 (30% of $50,000). Now $3,000 on our $15,000 hold is a pretty good one month return.

Writing calls is a great cash generation machine. So what's the down side? You're uncovered on the stock. The word "uncovered" is seldom used. The word used all the time is "naked," which means you have no underlying position on the stock. You're not covered.

The perceived risk of naked calls by your broker is huge. The actual risk can be dealt with quite easily. Let's explore this. You're okay if the stock stays below $50, and you're not okay if it goes above $50. If the stock shoots to $55 or $60, you might have to buy the stock at $55 to deliver it at $50. You would have a $5 or a $5,000 loss. Because of this your broker simply may not allow you to do this type of trade.

Tell your broker you want to place a "buy-stop" on the stock. A buy-stop is an order to purchase the stock at a certain price. So where should we place it? Remember that the stock has run up to $48. We do not start losing money until the stock gets above $53.

That was quite a leap in mathematical faith, so let me explain. We've agreed to sell the stock at $50 but we've taken in $3 of income. If we buy the stock at $53 and sell it for $50, we're at break-even because of the $3,000 premium we've previously received.

So, if we want to break-even, let's put the buy-stop at $53. If we want to keep the $3, then put the buy-stop at $50. We could wait for the stock to drop to say $46, and put the buy-stop at $48. I would not do this because we don't necessarily want to own the stock. If the stock drops to $48, just buy back the option and close the position. We could also place the buy-stop at $55 and be willing to lose $2,000! If it's volatile, you could end up buying the stock and then have it drop below $50 before you know it. Now you own the stock and it might not get called away. I'm not fond of losing money or taking any additional risk or loss potential. I place buy-stops at about the break even point.

If you have done your homework in the first place, the buy-stop will hardly ever be hit.

ANOTHER WAY

Is there another way to sell without owning the stock? Yes, and this will require an understanding of a second definition of the word "covered." Not only can you write covered calls by owning the stock; you could substitute the stock with an option to buy the stock. In the true sense of options investing, there is little difference in owning the stock or in having a right to buy the stock.

Let's see this at work. We'll keep using the previous example. If we sell the $50 call and don't want to own the stock or be in a naked position with the margin requirements, then let's buy the $45 calls.

The $45 calls are going for $6.50. To buy 10 contracts it will cost $6,500. That seems like a lot, but remember we sold or can sell the $50 call for $3. We spend $6,500 and take in $3,000. We have a cost now of $3,500 and what have we done? We've backed into a bull call spread. Note: This is not that good of a spread, which you'll figure out as we go along.

We have agreed to sell the stock at $50, but we have the right to buy the stock at $45. If the stock goes above $50 and we get called out, or have to sell, we make $5 (this is a $5 spread), or $5,000 minus what it cost us to create the spread. In this case, our cost is $3,500, so we net $1,500.

Remember the stock has to go above $50 for it to work perfectly. And think, in this example that was not our feeling. We thought the stock was hitting a peak at $48. You do bull call spreads when you think a stock is going up, not down.

WHAT IS A SPREAD?

A spread is created when you buy a call and sell a call on the same stock. In this case, we sold the $50 call and bought the $45 call.

Let me give a few thoughts about my system of spreads before we continue with definitions and examples.

The word "bull" means that you think a stock will go up or at least stay up above a particular strike price. With spreads we either spend money to create the spread or we take in money to create a spread. When we spend money it is called a "debit spread." When we take in money it is a "credit spread." With credit spreads we actually take money in and have it in our account the next day. The commitment lasts until the expiration date and the options expire or until we end it by buying back and closing the positions. I call this "winding out." We'll get to this topic later.

The word "bear" means that we think the stock is going down. Traditionally our brokers would get us involved in short sales or buying puts. But not Wade Cook. Short sales are too risky, and short sales and buying puts are too negative. They cause a negative personality change. I choose to bet on optimism, ride stocks up, and quit worrying about all the negative things.

Okay, back to our bull call spread. Let's look at the $40 call and the $45 call. We sold the $45 call for $6.50. In this different bull call spread the strike prices are the $40/$45. We could sell the $45 call for say $6. It costs $9.75 to buy the $40 call option.

Look at the numbers: (It's May 20)

June $40 call $9.50 x $9.75	Buy for $9,750
June $45 call = $6 x $6.5	Sell for $6,000
	Net cost $3,750

We sell the $45 call and buy the $40 call. Our net debit is $3.75. That's $3,750 of cost for a potential $1,250 profit. Now anytime we can get a $1,250 return on $3,750 we need to take a second look. But I'm sure that some of you are still having a hard time seeing the profit of $1,250 and the risk, or cost of $3,750. I've taught this at seminars many times and it is a tough one for some people. The $3,750 is derived by spending $9,750 and taking in $6,000. We are out of pocket $3,750. And remember, this is a one to four week play.

To help, let's forget the options for a while and just deal with the stock. If we buy 1,000 shares of stock at $40,000 and agree to sell the same stock for $45,000, we would have a $5,000 profit or gain (minus transaction costs). Why is it difficult to do it by proxy? We have the right to buy the stock at $40 and get paid hard cash for agreeing to sell it at $45. In this case, the option money out (money we spend) is offset by the money we take in. Our actual cost is $3,750. This much is spent to make what? We have a gross profit of $5,000, but our net profit is $1,250 ($5,000 spread profit minus our $3,750 cash invested = $1,250).

Our risk is the money we spent, or $3,750. We could lose all or part of this if the stock drops below $45. We can spend time on the numbers all day long and it might help some, however, at some point you just have to think: 10 contracts, hmmm; $5 call spread = $5,000. My cost is $3,750, my profit $1,250. Time of commitment four weeks–wow, not bad!

I don't need to know everything about a gas combustion engine to drive a car. Let's get in and go.

What About Dips

Remember we need the stock to go above and/or stay above the $45 strike price for this bull call spread to work 100%. If the stock goes below $45, we won't get called out. We then won't make the $5,000 cross profit. Yes, we can still buy back the $45 call immediately, and/or after waiting a bit longer, sell the $40 option we own.

This is winding out and it takes practice to get good at this. The most we can lose (even if the stock drops $20) is our $3,750. That is the total at risk. Should you sell on this dip or wait for the stock to go back up above the $45 price?

If the stock dips to $43 and you think that this is a new bottom with support then maybe you can put in place the $35 and $40 spread. This would give you a new profit potential.

This problem of dips leads me to the underlying situation that would get me excited about a bull call spread. We use a bullish strategy when we think or hope the stock is going up. We've done our homework. So even though I continued to use the first example of an uptick, or a peak in this stock ($42 up to $48) and I've tried to show you how to make money with this, it is important for you to realize these were for exercise purposes only. If we can make money in less than spectacular situations then how much can we make if we find a better playing field?

Let me say it simply. We do bull call spreads in a) a slightly in-the-money situation, when b) there is a high likelihood that the stock will rise. Again, we need to get called out, or exercised on to make the most money. In a bull put spread (BUPS), we don't want to get exercised on, but in a bull call spread (BUCS) we do. So if the stock is already above the strike price, there is a higher chance of getting called out.

One more example: A high-flying hi-tech stock had a steady incline. It's doing well. But it has fallen from $158 to $152. In this price range we may want to do a $10 spread. Okay, let's go slightly in the money. Let's buy the $140 call and sell the $150 call.

$140 calls = $14 x 14.50

$150 calls = $6 x 7

We buy the $140's for $14.50, or $14,500 and sell the $150 calls for $6, or $6,000. Our net cost is $8.50 times 1,000 or $8,500. That's what will also be on hold in our account, not 30% or so of $150,000 if we sold this uncovered. If the stock stays above $150, we will get called out and make $1,500. This is a 17% plus, one-month return.

Spend $14,500 and

Take in $6,000

                 $8,500 net cost, or net debit

                 $10,000 spread

                 -$8,500 net cost

                 $1,500 profit if the stock stays above $150

SUMMARY

- We do these spreads out of the money for protection.
- We do spreads to limit potential losses, to generate income (one to 31 days), and to lessen our margin requirement substantially.
- We do these spreads on dips hoping the stock goes up or stays up above $150. If the stock does so, we get called out and make maximum profits.

DOWNSIDE

You ask, with these incredible returns, can anything go wrong? Yes, but we've already shown you how to protect yourself by winding out of the position. We don't need to spend much time here, as we've covered wind-outs, and roll-ups, or roll-downs in other places. And more importantly, we won't have to spend much time or worry in real life if we do it right in the first place.

There is an aspect of bull call spreads that can seriously minimize your profits. It is the issue of broker's commissions. The problem is worse on E type of trading (electronic). You see, there are two sets of commissions going into the deal and two sets of commissions coming out of the deal. If you are called out, i.e.; the stock is above $150 in our last example then there is a new transaction to either sell the stock or exercise the option, and then buy the stock or exercise the option at the lower strike price.

I know I'm being a bit ambiguous because different brokers treat this differently. The second set of commissions could potentially be so high that I literally will not do a BUCS if the broker charges commissions on the second set. That's right, I ask for free commissions. They can charge (I hope you asked for and are getting preferential commissions on all your trades) on the first set—selling the $150 calls and buying the $140 calls. But that's it. If they want to charge $40 to $80 to get exercised it might not be too bad, but some say you have a commission on the stock purchase of $150,000 and $140,000. Some get away with it. Technically, this may be what happens but they can and should substitute the option for the stock.

Some brokers have available SDS or Same Day Substitution wherein they use the proxy side, or options, to fulfill your stock obligation. Some say this is hogwash, and to them maybe it is because they're not up with the better trading systems. It's not worth arguing about because either way—stock or options—you don't want to pay commissions. Tell them you're a "meter drop" kind of person. More deals, more spreads, more money to them. You, after all, are the one that has to be profitable. If you pay $80 to put the two options in place, and $300 and $400 to sell the $150 stock and buy the $140 stock, that's $780 of cost off your $1,250 profit. It's not worth it.

They'll do it your way if they want your business. You'll just have to educate them about the potential.

DEBIT/CREDIT SPREADS

A bull call spread and a bear put spread are debit spreads in that we expend money to put these in place. Both of these spreads may potentially require two sets of commissions. Bull put spreads and bear call spreads, my two favorites, are credit spreads. We take in money, and they only have one set of commissions. At expiration the options just expire, with no second set of commissions.

Debit Spreads = Two sets of commission (4)

Credit Spreads = One set of commissions (2)

Don't give up on BUCS though because a good broker, who works effectively, can help you make a lot of money.

HIGH FLYERS

Spreads can sometimes work when the stock is way out of the money, or way in the money compared to the strike price. Remember there's a lot of volatility to some stocks and options; therefore, they have high premiums. High premiums usually mean high profit. The risk is also higher.

TWENTY CONTRACT SPREADS

First of all, options market makers love spreads. They have a buyer and a seller in place. I don't know all of their reasons, maybe it's the two commissions, maybe it's working with two "in the spread" variables; I just don't know. But I hear everywhere that these are their favorites.

Also, they (the brokers and the market makers) like doing these spreads in 20 contract increments. I know my examples here are 10 contracts, that is for the ease of the math. In real life, try to do 20 at a time. That will double the risk, double the hold amount, and double the profits.

Don't get me wrong, if you can only afford three contracts, go for it. But the preferred number is 20. Many times I'll do 40.

WHY SLIGHTLY OUT OF THE MONEY?

We do our homework and we're ready to pounce. We have to choose our strike prices. We'll go to a new example to show you this feature. A stock is down from $72 to $62, a $10 drop. There are a bunch of option strike prices and premiums. These are all for the next month out.

The $50 call = 12   x   12.50

The $55 call = 8   x   9

The $60 call = 5   x   5.25

The $65 call = 2   x   2.25

The riskiest spread would be the $60/$65. Nice money. It's risky because the stock has to go above $65 to get called out.

Look at the numbers:

Buy the $60 call for $5.25, or $5,250

Sell the $65 call for $2.00, or $2,000

We net debit (spend) $3.25, or $3,250

Our profit will be $5,000 minus the $3,250, or $1,750. We will make $1,750 on $3,250, but remember the stock must go above $65, and it might not do that. This is a great return, over 50% for one month, but very risky. If we don't get called out the options either expire and we lose the $3,250, or we buy back the option we sold (hence, ending the obligation) and sell the option we previously purchased for whatever we can get.

We don't want risk, so let's move down one strike price.

Buy the $55 call for $9, or $9,000

Sell the $60 call for $5, or $5,000

We net debit (spend) $4, or $4,000

We spend $4 to make $1. Still a good 25% return for one month, but look at the padding or protection. The stock is $2 above the strike price of $60. We have $2 for protection, and it was on a dip.

Now as we move down to the next set of strike prices, you'll see the profits vanish, but so does most of the risk.

Buy the $50 call for $12.50, or $12,500

Sell the $55 call for $8.00, or $8,000

Our profit is just $0.50 or $4,500 debit (or cost).

Five thousand dollar spread potential, but a net cost of $4,500. $4,500 (which we'll get back) to make $500 is okay; it's 11% for a month, but not a great return. It's almost a sure thing though. Our $62 stock, which is heading up, just needs to stay above $55.

Why is this lower set of strike prices less risky and less profitable? Simply stated, without a lot of time, most of the option price is in the money, or the intrinsic value portion of the option. There is not a lot of fluff in these premiums.

CONCLUSION

Bull call spreads normally work well when done slightly in the money, or in other words, just above the highest strike price, and *always when the stock is heading up.*

Practice, regroup, and practice

As you say, I am honoured and famous and rich. But as I have to do all the hard work, and suffer an increasing multitude of fools gladly, it does not feel any better than being reviled, infamous and poor, as I used to be.

George Bernard Shaw

CHAPTER 10

SELLING PUTS FOR INCOME GENERATION

At the time of this writing, doing bull put spreads is my favorite strategy. Hands down, it's my most frequently used formula. Some weeks I'll do 10 to 15 bull put spreads to every one other strategy. Yes, that's all of them combined. One of the reasons for this will probably surprise you, if you don't know me very well. I'll get to this reason later–after I explain this type of play and try to let you figure it out.

We need to set this up. We'll explore the basic sell put strategy as outlined in Chapters 3 through 7 of *Stock Market Miracles*. We'll also deal with slams, dips, or other motivating factors as a determinant of when to employ this strategy. When this chapter is over you'll see all three strategies combined. I'm excited to share this with you and hope you learn and earn a lot.

THE BASIC SELL PUT STRATEGY

In the stock market the word "write" means to sell. Writing covered calls means selling a call on a covered position. When we sell, we take in money. Writing puts or selling puts is a way of generating cash. It requires you to take on an obligation and you get paid for this. Let's look at a pure put play from the buy side. If a stock has run up from $72 to $78 and you think this new price is unsustain-

able, you could buy the $80 put (or the $75 put). You have purchased the right, not the obligation, to put (sell) this stock to someone else. As the stock comes down the value of your put increases.
Look at the comparison of stock to put price in this illustration:

STOCK PRICE	$75 PUT PRICE	$80 PUT PRICE
$78	$4	$3.00
$76	$5	$5.50
$74	$6	$8.00
$70	$9	$11.50

You can see that as the stock moves down, the value of your put
moves up. There is a corresponding (and somewhat magnified)
move in the option. This movement partially depends on the time
remaining until the expiration, plus the "implied volatility" of the
option. If you had purchased the $75 put at $4, for 10 contracts you
would have tied up $4,000 (and control 1,000 shares of stock–one
contract is 100 shares). A few weeks later you could sell the put for
$6,000, on the stock sliding down to $74. That's a $2,000 profit.

Now if the stock goes up to say $80, your $4 put could easily go
down to $2. If the stock doesn't retreat you could lose $2 or $2,000.
That's if you sell it. If you hang on you could lose the whole $4,000
if the stock continues to rise or stays above $80. Obviously, when we
buy puts we hope the stock goes down in a timely manner so the
option will go up.

It's this rise in stock price that I'd like to zero in on. Does it pique
your interest? I'll explain this in detail as we go on, but let me pose
a new angle for many of you. What if we think the stock is going up
from $76? Let's sell the $75 put instead of buying it (that's $5,000).
That would generate income. Then as the stock rises to $78 we
could "buy back" this put for $4,000 and keep the $1,000 profit. We
could also let it ride and buy it for $1 as the stock goes much high-
er. Spend $1,000 and keep our $3,000 profit (less transaction costs).
If we want to wait up to the third Friday of the expiration month it
will just expire and we would keep the whole $4,000 (LTC).

That was simple but we need to explore this strategy in more detail so we can a) make money and b) keep out of trouble.

THE GOOD, THE BAD, THE UGLY

Writing puts is another way of saying writing naked puts, or writing uncovered puts. We have no position on the underlying stock. By selling an option we have opened a position on the underlying stock–this position is a current obligation to do something. That something is our obligation to purchase the stock at an agreed upon price. Now the only way a stock will get put to you, at say $75, is if the stock is below $75, or even at $75 in some rare cases.

Think of it. No one will sell you the stock at $75 if it's going for $78. If however the stock drops to $73 or $70 you will get it put to you. On Monday after the third Friday you will find out if you are the proud owner of the stock.

TAKING STOCK

A few random thoughts about getting stock put to you:

1. Many people sell puts as a way of buying the stock at a discount. Go back to our example. If you sold the $75 put for $2, or 10 contracts for $2,000, and now take the stock at $75, or $75,000, your actual cost basis is $73,000 or $73 per share. You use the option premium received to adjust the cost basis downward. Think it through–if you later sell the stock for $80,000 your gain will be $7,000.

2. You should never sell puts on a stock unless you want to own it. I do not sell puts to buy the stock. I sell puts to generate immediate income, wait for a decrease in value of the put and either buy it back or let it expire.

3. Remember that these are American style options. They can be exercised any time on or before the expiration date. If you sell a $75 put on January 20 with a February 17 expiration date and the stock dips to $73; the next Tuesday, or any other date before February 17th, all of the stock or part of it could get put to you. This is rare.

The point to remember is that you've taken on an obligation to perform. That's why you get the big bucks. Now in real life, depending on the stock, volatility, and length of time to expiration, puts can be very expensive. I've seen some $75 puts, when the stock is at $78, go for $8 to $13. Think of these larger premiums, $8,000, or $13,000 in our 10-contract example: Nice income, but you still have the obligation to buy the stock at $75. These are not only nice premiums or income, but also would adjust the basis nicely downward if the stock is put to you.

THE DOWNSIDE

It is not uncommon to generate 15 to 30% monthly returns by selling puts. So what is the downside? The downside of writing puts is the same as owning the stock. It's all the way to zero. Before you get the stock put to you, or even after, the stock could fall out of bed. Your $78 stock could drop to $68 or $28 or $8. Now obviously this rarely happens and even if the stock dips you are not devoid of opportunities for a come back and cash flow while it's happening. You could wait it out. You could sell at a loss and re-deploy your money elsewhere. You could write covered calls on your new stock at various strike prices to generate income while it's coming back up. We make a lot of money selling puts, but before I once again incur the wrath of the so-called market gurus and tell you how much we've made, or how many successful deals in a row we do or how many out of the 80 to 120 transactions we do a month are successful, I'll invite you to look at W.I.N.™ at wadecook.com. Go there and see each deal done. You can go back one week and get all my trades, or even a month and see how well we do. To all my critics, I'm arming you with facts. See how you deal with the truth. Tell me anyone who puts all their trades on an Internet site.

Why do brokers frown on your doing these types of trades? A few observations, one or more just might apply to your stockbroker:

1. Bless their hearts, stockbrokers just can't keep up with all these strategies. Many know nothing of selling puts or bull put spreads.

2. Some stockbrokers are new and even though they have down the basics to do certain trades, their firm may have policies against new brokers doing these plays. But, it's always your fault–your lack of experience, or your small amount of cash.

3. Without getting too simplistic, the form you fill out to trade tells a story in and of itself. The question is what type of trading would you like to do, and sometimes how much experience you have with each type of trade. The list starts off with buy and sell stocks and mutual funds, then on to writing covered calls, then buy call and put options (and maybe a few more), but last or close to last is "sell naked puts." My feeling is that it should be up around two or three, but it's at the bottom, signifying the riskiest of all. Sad, but true that selling puts gets placed last on this list.

I'd like to take off here and use this last point to jump into bull put spreads, but there is another important point to be made. It's essential that you understand margin requirements, premium hold, and how it changes. Once this is over bull put spreads will shine.

MARGIN: A MOVING TARGET

When we take on the obligation to take the stock, our brokers will make us keep a certain amount of cash on hand. Some of this is called margin. Remember margin is a type of debt in stock purchases. In writing uncovered calls, selling puts and credit spreads (bull put spreads and bear call spreads), it's the amount your brokerage firm puts on hold until your obligation is complete–usually at the expiration date.

Let's use the same example, write the $75 put and see where it takes us. Again we'll use 10 contracts. Sell for $4, or $4,000. That $4,000 comes from the market; it is in your account the next day, but you absolutely cannot spend it. It's on hold until the position ends. It's not margin hold but it is on hold.

Now on to the margin part. There are two calculations to determine how much will be on hold. It's an either/or situation– whichever is greater. (Quick note: your broker can require more if they choose. This is from the Federal SEC guidelines and literally all of the brokers I know follow this exactly.)

1. You will have to hold on margin 20% of the stock price, with an adjustment for any out-of-the-money portion.

   a. Multiply 20% x $78,000 = $15,600

b. Minus $3,000 (out of the money) $3,000 is the amount above the strike price of $75

c. This is $12,600 on hold, for margin

d. Plus the $4,000 premium received

e. Equals $16,600 on hold ($4,000 + $12,600 margin)

Not bad. A potential profit of $4,000 on $16,600. That's a 24% monthly return. In calculating the rate of return, you don't have to use the $4,000 premium hold as it is not your money, and $4,000 divided by $12,600 is even better. But we don't want to make this look too good.

(or) 2. Ten percent of the stock price (plus the premium), with no adjustments.

a. Take 10% of $78,000 = $7,800

b. Plus the $4,000 premium

c. Equals $11,800 total on hold

Remember it's whichever is greater. In this case it would be $16,600 from calculation 1.

DOES IT CHANGE?

I'm glad you asked, because it surely does. As the stock moves up or down your broker's computers are whirring away in the middle of the night figuring out your new margin requirements. If the stock price rises, you could free up margin and do something else with this "added" buying power. If the stock moves down, it will tie up more margin. They might even ask you to bring in more money. Remember, showing you this is to keep you out of trouble.

Let's see what happens if the stock moves down. And think it through, if the stock drops below $75 the likelihood that you'll get the stock put to you increases. Naturally, they will want more money in the account to help out with the obligation. The stock drops to $72.

Here we go again:

1. Twenty percent of the stock price, or $14,200, minus any out-of-the-money portion. Whoa. It's not out of the money any more; it's now in the money by $3 or $3,000. You subtract a negative so it becomes a positive (-) -$3,000 or add $3,000. The new amount on hold is $17,200. Plus (don't forget the $4,000 premium) $4,000 + $17,200 = $21,200 on hold.

Wow! Our margin (plus premium) has gone from $16,600 to $21,200. (Note: Make sure you keep enough cash on hand to cover margin calls. Maybe you should have only done five contracts or eight contracts.)

(or) 2. Ten percent of $72 or $72,000 is $14,400 plus the $4,000 premium. Total on hold = $18,400.

Again, it's the greater of #1 or #2–#1 is $21,200. The #2 calculation won't kick in until the stock rises, as we shall soon see.

Now, however, what if the stock rises? Happy days are here again. Up we go, to say $87. Can you guess that our margin requirements will go down? Let's do the numbers:

1. Twenty percent
   a. Take 20% of $87,000 = $17,400
   b. Minus any out-of-the-money portion, or $12,000 ($87,000 is $12,000 out of the money on a $75 put strike price)
   c. Now $17,400 - $12,000 = $5,400 on hold
   d. Plus the $4,000 (premium) = $9,400 on hold

Now look, our $16,600 original hold (when we first sold the option) is now down to $9,400. That's $7,200 ($16,600 - $9,400) available for other things. Or is it? Don't forget B.

(or) 2. Ten percent of $87,000 is $8,700, plus the $4,000 premium = $11,700 on hold.

This time #2 is larger. Yes, it's still down from the $16,600 but not as low as $9,400. You see, the 10% is a catch. You could have the premium so far out of the money that the margin hold would be close to zero (except for the premium hold). The 10% makes you keep something on hold.

WHAT IF THE STOCK GOES DOWN?

Now, we've discussed margin but what about the lower stock. Should you ever let it get put to you?

After a previous statement that the stock could get put to you at any time before the expiration date, that last question must seem strange. How can you stop it?

This is a difficult thing to understand. I don't understand exactly how the computers work, but the generalized mechanism I do.

1. In order for a stock to get put to you, someone has to exercise and put the stock. Most people don't put the stock. They just sell their put at a profit (hopefully).

2. Next there is a rotation or order to things. It's random and is by computer choice. Yes, in theory, if the stock is at $72 and the strike price is at $75 it could get put to you at any time, but since most options are exercised on the expiration date, it gives you plenty of time to get out.

3. It just takes a few seconds to sell. If your $4,000 is down to $3,000, the sell is easy. Remember that sometimes the stock and options bounce back. You only did the strategy when you thought the stock was going up. If it goes south, either sell for a loss, wait it out, or sell and roll out.

Before I deal with buybacks and roll outs let's explore "eroding premiums" and see how we might not lose that much money–eventually we will probably still win. This is a tough one for many Americans because they just don't see how they can make money when the stock drops.

In our example, I think most see how to make money on a falling stock if you own the put, but not if you sold the put.

Okay, let's shake things up a bit. When you sold the $75 put your premium of $4 was all time value. Nothing becomes intrinsic value or in the money until the stock dips below $75. Now what if the stock drops to $73. If it does so quickly, the premium you sold for $4 could become $7 or so. What if the drop is slow–so slow that we get near the expiration date. What will happen to the premium?

DATE	STOCK PRICE	OPTION PRICE($75 PUT)
Jan. 19	$78	$4
Jan. 21	$73	$7

To end this position it would cost $7,000 and we'd lose $3,000. In a few paragraphs I'll show you how to turn this negative into a positive. But our discussion here is about eroding premiums.

Here, the stock drops to $73, but we're getting close to expiration. The stock starts to go back up but does not get above $75.

DATE	STOCK PRICE	OPTION PRICE($75 PUT)
Feb. 10	$73.00	$7.00
Feb. 12	$73.50	$5.00
Feb. 14	$74.00	$4.00
Feb. 17	$74.50	$2.50
Feb. 18	$74.75	$.50

How can this be? The stock is still below the strike price. Why haven't the options gone up more? The premium has eroded immensely. Remember the option premium is made up of time value. As the time disappears the premium also disappears.

Well, what do we do? On February 17, we could buy the 10 contracts for $2.50 or $2,500. We could sell them for $4,000, that's a $1,500 profit. What does buy back mean? Obviously "buy back" is stock market jargon. If you buy a call or a put it shows up on your account statement. If you then sell it, you would be selling the same call with the strike price and the same expiration date. The buy and the sell transactions cancel each other out.

What about the opposite? You sell first and then go in and buy the same position. To the computer it's a wash. So to buy back means that we're buying the same option (strike price and expiration date) and closing out the position.

In this example we're buying it back for less money than we sold it for. We keep the profit. Now this won't always happen. But it does frequently, and it happens often when you sell out-of-the-money puts. I like that extra pad of $3 ($78 vs. $75 strike price) and do this on dips when there's a high likelihood the stock will go up.

You Can't Lose

Are you ready for a bunch of safety? We just said that if the stock goes down, you could buy it back and end the position. That costs money, but what the put costs this month can always be sold for more next month. I'm not saying you should roll out but you can. You may want to just end the position and take your marbles somewhere else. But if you think the stock has really hit bottom, sell the next month's put at the same or the next lower strike price.

Back to our example: we sold the $75 put for $4. The stock drops to $72. It might cost us $5 to buy it back and we would be underwater by $1, or $1,000. Now, check the $75 put for next month. It's going for $6.50. Selling it would generate $6,500 and we're back making money. The stock is $72; the strike price is $75. If we want more safety, sell the $70 put for $3,000 or the $65 put for $1,000. Either way we're profitable again and have moved down a strike price or two.

I love it when we can't lose. Let's go once more. You sell the $70 put for $3, or $3,000. The $1,000 hole you were in has evaporated and you're up $2,000. You're sure the stock will go up but it doesn't. It drops below $70. Buy it back and end it—even at a loss, or buy it back and roll out to the next month once again.

You see you can keep doing this until the stock turns around and starts heading back up. It may be clear down to $50 by then but you've made money all the way down and now as it turns up, you're really profitable.

You can't lose at selling puts with this buy back and roll out feature. Try it on paper. I'll bet you can't lose at it. This is the only stock market strategy I've ever found where you can't lose.

Summary

- A quick review. Selling puts generates income. You get paid for taking on an obligation. Because you have an obligation, some money is held in your account. This amount fluctuates.

- Selling puts lets you buy at a discount. If the stock stays above the strike price you get to keep the cash.

- Dips in the stock create a temporary problem, but these problems can be overcome. As you learn the added advantages of doing bull put spreads, I think you'll cease to wonder why this is my favorite cash flow power strategy.

- And before I end, I've just started my N.E.W. (Never Ending Wealth) nationwide seminars on these topics. Call 1-800-872-7411 and get the schedule.

Success in life is a matter not so much
of talent or opportunity as of
concentration and perseverance.

Charles William Wendte

CHAPTER 11

BULL PUT SPREADS

One of the things that consumes me is finding ways to avoid losing money. In fact it is my passion. The tens of thousands of people who have attended and benefited from my seminars and workshops appreciate this drive for cash flow profits.

It is really important to me. One reason is because it's not only important to others, it is essential. Why? Unlike these huge fund managers and "stock market experts," some of my students only have a few thousand dollars to get started. If I taught events only to people who have over $1,000,000 or even $100,000, my ideas would probably more closely coincide with theirs.

It is comical to read their criticisms of me. Funny that they do not know of or have not heard of these strategies. My goodness, anyone can look on our Internet site and see virtually all of my trades. In fact, I would love to have a discussion or debate over implementation of formulas. Which formula works when and where? But no, they just want to dig up garbage that has no basis in reality, et cetera, et cetera.

I don't want to belabor this point, but I feel it is necessary at the beginning of this chapter. You see, this is my favorite formula. I have a passion for it. This strategy has helped thousands "cash flow" their investments. Oh, it's not a high flyer. It will not make anyone rich overnight. If you want a $10 stock to turn into $100 by sundown tonight or in a year, this is not the place to read.

This strategy is about protection and cash flow. It's about taking the best there is, in knowledge of the market option plays, in leveraged movements and in generating predictable returns. As I've stated from my first book, these formulas are for cash flow generation. It's not about equity, but cash. You can buy extra equities or other investments with this cash. You can buy gold or groceries, it's your money.

In this chapter LTC = less transaction costs. The returns mentioned are monthly returns. We do bull put spreads out about one month. Every position will expire in one to 31 days. Over and out. If we're profitable, it's time to reinvest or go to the movies. If we're not so profitable or we lose, the position is also over. Our losses will be minimal and we'll know the potential loss and profits before we get involved. How's that for a new thought? We can measure our risk and reward from minute one.

Now as I've said from my early real estate days, until now, if you know exactly how much you're going to make on a deal, you're not going to make that much. Not making a huge cash gain is okay for some people. Some want a steady, predictable cash flow. Let's start with $20,000. If $20,000 generates about $4,000 to $5,000 per month would that be good? Some want more. If you are one of those who want millions on every deal, stop and go to another one of my books and study pure options plays or bottom fishing stocks or IPOs. Today, Internet stocks would be a place to go for potentially extraordinary returns on way overvalued and risky stocks.

Okay. Are you still here? If so, let's get on to 20% monthly "real cash flow" returns.

DEFINITIONS

We can't do spreads without understanding the components. So a few words need to be defined. There are many different types of spreads. Actually four that the average person can do with much repeatable success. There are also variations and combinations.

A spread is created when you sell an option and buy an option on the same stock with:

1. Different strike prices.
2. The same strike price but different expiration dates.
3. Different strike prices and different expiration dates.

If we purchase and own an $85 call option and sell the $90 call option, this would create a $5 spread. This is a bull call spread. This one is similar to writing a covered call. We have agreed to sell our stock (controlled by the $90 call). If the stock is above $90 and we get "called out" we exercise the $85 call and deliver the stock. Actually our options will substitute for the stock.

If we own 10 contracts, the most we would make would be $5,000 minus what we paid for the $85 call and what we took in by selling the $90 call. It's like buying the stock for $85,000 and selling for $90,000. Do you see the $5,000 profit? If it cost us a "net debit" (what we paid to buy and sell the call) of $3,750, our profit would be $1,250 (LTC). See Chapter 8 about bull call spreads.

Now, you must be wondering why I would bring up bull call spreads here in a chapter about bull put spreads. It's because sometimes the way to understand something is to compare it to something else. Many Americans have a problem understanding put options. Most people have no problem with calls. Hence the set up with a bull call spread for the comparison later.

BULL AND BEAR

When we use the word "bear" in front of a strategy, as in bear call spreads (my second favorite formula) and bear put spreads it simply means we think the stock (or the market as a whole) will go down or at least stay the same.

The opposite is true with the use of the word bull. Bull strategies contemplate or hope that a stock will go up or at least stay up above a certain strike price.

BULL PUT SPREADS

Let's do one:

We see that ABC Company has dipped down, or is expected to come out with great numbers or whatever. We think it's going up.

The stock is at $92, down from a high of $99. It seems to have found good support at $91. We call our broker and sell the $90 put. We buy the $85 put at the same time. In fact this is a married position. We have created a $5 spread. For this and all other examples in this chapter we'll use 10 contracts. The math is easier. (Note: In real life you should try to do at least 20 contracts at a time. More on this later.)

What have we done? We sold the $90 puts, for let's say $2.50, or $2,500. We have taken on an obligation to buy 1,000 shares of this stock at $90. Now, remember from the chapter on selling naked puts, there is risk and an obligation. The downside of selling puts naked or uncovered is tremendous, unless we wind out of the position. As long as the stock stays above $90 we will be just fine. Also remember most stockbrokers won't let you do naked sells and remember also that there is a margin requirement, or hold in your account.

Okay, with all this to remember and with all your thinking about the risk and margin, simply buy the $85 put. Let's pay $1 or $1,000. I hope you see the $1,500 cash flow into your account. We get this by selling the $90 put for the $2,500 and paying out $1,000 to buy the $85 put. It gives us a net credit of $1,500 (LTC).

We have put in place a $5 bull put spread. Let's see what we have done.

1. By spending the money and purchasing the $85 put we have limited our downside risk. By limiting this risk we have assuaged our brokers fears. He will let us do this, where he wouldn't let us do a pure put sell. No kidding, you walk in and say, "I want to sell a (naked) put." He won't let you. Walk back in and say "I want to do a bull put spread on that same stock." And he'll say, "Sit down. How many contracts?"

Why is this so? Remember the risk. Our downside is now limited by spending the $1,000 on the $85 put. We have purchased insurance. If the stock falls, the value of the $85 put which we own would go up in value, compensating for the loss of value in the stock.

2. Now, not only can we do this but also our margin requirement has been seriously diminished. In fact, here's what our margin becomes. It's the amount of the spread minus the net credit. With 10 contracts we've created a $5,000 spread. But the market gave us $1,500 of this so all we have to keep on hold is about $3,500 ($5,000 minus $1,500 income = $3,500). *Are you getting excited?*

3. We have limited our downside loss risk to the $3,500 on hold. Our risk is the whole $5,000. We could lose this $5,000 if the stock really drops below $85. But the $5,000 total potential loss is offset by the $1,500 we took in, hence our loss can only be $3,500 (LTC).

4. Just because the stock takes a dip into dangerous territory we're not devoid of strategies to cut our losses. If the stock is at $88 or lower, depending on the time left, we could unwind the position, simultaneously or in two phases. Here's how this works. Buy back the $90 put, and sell the $85 put. The $90 put could cost us, say even $1,500 and we'll get 25¢ for selling the $85 put, hopefully $250. Well, there goes our profit. The $1,250 we spend edges out the $1,500 we made. We're slightly underwater at this time.

5. We were able to measure our risk of $3,500, and our reward of $1,500 before we entered the spread. In fact we should shop around to find the best candidates. Here's what makes a good sound spread.

    a. The stock is a well-known big company. It makes a lot of money.

    b. It has positive news or is in a steady uptrend or on a brief dip.

    c. The premiums work. You shop and get the deal right for you.

Look at this rate of return: divide $1,500 by the $3,500 amount on hold (our risk amount) for one, two or four weeks. That's a 42% plus return.

Let's do another one. A huge computer software company is expected to have great earnings and have even hinted at a stock split. The stock is up from $120 three months ago to $145. You expect it to and hope it will go much higher.

Check out the $140 put and the $135 put. From $25 to the $200 stock prices, strike prices are in $5 increments. Above $200 the strike prices are in $10 intervals. I like $5 spreads. Under $25 I do $2.50 spreads. On more expensive stocks I do $10 or even $20 spreads. And even though the price area around $150 has $5 intervals strike prices, I still do $10 spreads in this price range.

The $140 put is going for $9. We take in $9,000. The $135 put is $7. We'll spend $7,000 with a net credit of $2,000. We make $2,000 as long as the stock stays above $140. Not much profit, but $2,000 for one month or less on a $3,000 hold is not bad. The $3,000 hold is the $5,000 spread differential minus the $2,000 we netted by selling the $9,000 put and buying the $7,000 put. Rate of return equals 60% for the month, or the two weeks or so this spread is in place– $2,000/$3,000 = 50% plus, rate of return.

Now, these are pretty high premiums, a lot of fluff, and why? Because of the high volatility, or what many call "implied volatility." When there are wide swings, either up or down, option premiums can get very expensive. Let's look at a more normal situation.

Same stock price and same strike prices. If the stock is at $145 the $140 put usually goes for around $2.50 and the $135 put for $1. Okay? Let's sell 10 contracts of the $140 put and buy 10 contracts of the $135. Income is $2,500, expense is $1,000, and we net $1,500. Our hold will be $3,500. A $1,500 profit with $3,500 on hold is a nice 40% plus return for say, two weeks.

Put It In Place—How Tos

You do your homework, you watch a stock. You are certain it's going up and then call your stockbroker. Now:

1. Tell them how you want to do a bull put spread on XYZ stock at the $140/$135 put strike prices.

2. Try to do 20 contracts at a time. Option market makers love spreads. They sell both sides of a position and they like that. Twenty contract groups go to the head of the class. In the above example it would take $7,000 in your account to do 20 contracts.

3. Doing 20 contracts can cut down the costs, or increase your income if you get a little better deal. You see if the options market maker is placing 20 + 20 contracts, they can work the deal for a better return for you. They can buy or sell one position in the spread—between the bid and ask.

For example, the $140 put is going for $2.50 x $2.75 ($2½ x $2¾) and the $135 put is bid and ask at $1.25 x $1.50 ($1¼ x $1½). There is some play here. Even a $⅛ better deal will make you an extra $250 on the 20 contracts. Now instead of making $3,000 ($1,500 x 2 or x 20 contracts) you now make $3,250 on a $6,750 hold instead of $3,000 on a $7,000 hold. The rate of return increases commensurately.

Another way to do this is to tell your broker you want a net credit of $1,625 for 10 or $3,250 for 20 contracts. Actually you can just say you want a $1⅝ net credit. Now you may not get it right away. Maybe it takes a slight downturn in the stock. Be a little patient and bam, you get filled at this better price.

SLIGHTLY OUT OF THE MONEY

You have an obligation to take this stock at $140. You have left a $5 cushion between the current stock price of $145 and your obligation strike price of $140. You're completely safe as long as the stock stays above $140.

Now take a look at the $140/$145 put. We will make more money, but also increase our risk. Simply put, for us to make maximum money we don't want the stock to be put to us. If we do the $140/$145 put, there is a higher likelihood the stock will get put to us. You see, the stock staying above $140 carries a certain risk, but there is much more risk if we need the stock to stay above $145.

Let's look at the numbers:

The $140 put = 2\frac{1}{2}$ x 2\frac{3}{4}$

The $145 put = 4\frac{3}{4}$ x $5

If we do it at the market, we'll sell the $145 put for 4\frac{3}{4}$ and buy the $140 put for 2\frac{3}{4}$. This would be a $5 spread netting us $2, or $2,000 for 10 contracts and $4,000 net for 20 contracts; $4,000 paid to you from the marketplace and $6,000 of your money on hold (20 contracts). This is a 60% monthly return. Why don't you put down this chapter right now and call your broker. Shop around and see what you find. You'll be amazed. You can see that if you were to just sell the put without buying the underlying strike price put, that you'd make more money—you wouldn't be spending the extra money to buy the lower put, but your margin requirement is so much more. In fact you can sometimes pull off two to three spreads for the margin requirement of 20% or so of the $140 stock, or about $28,000. Margin requirement can sometimes be more.

Think of this. You've limited your downside, you can precalculate your return, and you've seriously diminished your hold or margin requirement. You see why I like bull put spreads so much?

Okay, you say, what is the downside, no matter the fact that your losses would be limited?

What If The Stock Goes Down?

If the stock dips a little it might not matter if it recovers and goes back up above the strike price. However, if it sags below the strike price and especially if we're getting close to the expiration date, then we probably need to wait. We need to end the position, at least the topside, or the obligation side of the spread. In this example, the $145 put which we sold.

Let's wind out. Simply, we buy back the $145 put. Even if we lose $500 or $1,500 it might be better to end the position at a loss than to take the stock. Now remember our total loss can only be $3,000. (That's $5,000 on a 10 contract deal minus the $2,000 of outside income.) If we can spend even $1,500 to end the position we'd still make $500–$2,000 original profit minus this new expense of $1,500–and we might be able to sell the $140 puts for 25¢ or 50¢. That would add back in $250 or $500.

So a complete wind out would be to do everything in reverse. Wherein we sold the $145 put and bought the $140 put we would now buy the $145 put and sell the $140 put. We would close all positions. You can do these simultaneously or one at a time. You may not sell the $140 put first. If you do, you would be in a "naked" position and most of your stockbrokers won't let you do this.

Okay, winding out or buying back may be a bummer. So, let's throw back in some excitement and roll down and do it again on the next set of lower strike prices.

If our original position is the $140/$145 put spread, and if we think the $142 or $143 stock price is a good new support level, then create a spread on the $135/$140 put. We might be able to even get $1.50 or $2 as a credit. That would add to our profits if we're profitable or lessen our losses if we're a little underwater.

Let me reiterate a comment I made about not losing money in my sell put strategy (Chapter 10). If you play this right, by buying back and rolling out to the next month, or down to the next strike price levels, you can't lose. Try it on paper, you can't lose. You can always buy back a position this month and sell it for more next month. You can also buy back a position and sell it for about the same amount of money at lower strike prices.

As of this writing, Yahoo! had just announced a stock split. The stock before the split was bouncing everywhere. Yesterday it was at $342. The $290/$300 bull put spread netted me $1⅝, or $1,625. I did 20 contracts for $3,250. It is a $10 spread so $16,750 is on hold for about three weeks. I'll make $3,250 as long as the stock stays above $300. It is a good calculated risk as the stock is $42 out of the money. I like bull put spreads.

A Post From W.I.N.™

The following is an excerpt from W.I.N.™ (The Wealth Information Network™) and an example of information that I regularly post to our web site:

Good morning, this is Wade.

This is an interesting day of playing basketball, but a more inter-esting day once I got back in the car.

An unusual thing happened with expiration date on Friday. This is the first day, Monday, after the expiration date for March 1999. FDX Corporation (FDX), the parent company of Federal Express, had announced a 2:1 stock split a few days before expiration, and we had put in place 40 contracts of the $90/$95 bull put spread. In doing a bull put spread, we are hoping to make a certain amount of money based on a net credit, or money that we make by selling the $95 puts and buying the $90 puts in this example. We made $1/2 in this $5 spread, which means that we had $18,000 on hold or tied up in margin in our account to make $2,000. And it was just a three-day play, so that in and of itself is a nice return.

Here is the unusual thing that happened. The stock today opened up at $96 1/4, and shortly after the open, we found out that we had 1,000 shares of the stock put to us at the $95 price. Since we had 40 contracts, we could have had up to 4,000 shares put to us, but the computer only assigned us 1,000. Remember, in a spread position, you still have an obligation. In a bull call spread, you would have an obligation on the upper strike price call that you sold, in a bull put spread, you have an obligation to have put to you the stock at a certain strike price if the stock is below the strike price. Or so one would think. In this case here, the stock was above the $95 strike price, so in theory, there is no way that this stock should have gotten put to us. But it did.

Now here are a few thoughts. If the stock is at or near the strike price, there is always a chance of getting called out on a covered call basis, or having the stock put to you on a short put position. However, once again, this stock was really not that close, in that it was at $96 at the close on Friday, and opened up at $96 1/4 on the open on Monday. What we did, was immediately sell the stock for $96 1/4, which means on the 1,000 shares we made an extra $1 1/4, or $1,250 less transaction costs on selling the stock that we purchased this morning on having it put to us.

How could this happen? Remember the stock market closes at 4:00 PM Eastern Time, and for all intents and purposes for buying and selling options the options market closes at 4:04 or 4:05 PM Eastern Time. However, the options market is open until 5:00 PM Eastern Time for the execution or exercising of options. Let me reiterate this, to buy and sell an option, you have about the time the stock market closes, and a few minutes plus. But to exercise an option, you have a whole hour after the market closes. So if you want to exercise a call or exercise a put you can do so up to one hour afterwards. And I am not sure of this, that you can even do it afterwards if you can find a mechanism or a process to contact either a trading person or an OCC (Options Clearing Corporation) person to even have it exercised after that time. However, for functionality, I think that when the options market closes one hour after the stock market trading will be about the last time that you can actually trade or exercise your option. Now, remember the options market does not really close until Saturday after the third Friday of the month. But for that one-hour period you could exercise your option.

Now, here is just a surmising of what could have happened on Friday. Someone, who owned the stock or was in a long position on the put side of the Federal Express stock, did not want it and possibly thought that the stock would open down. Maybe they had some bad information, because the stock obviously opened up, but with this information they decided that they did not want to own the stock and exercised the put option. Now, this has happened to me in the last several years, one or two times. But this is a good example right now to have you learn the difference between buying and selling options and exercising options after the market closes. So somebody out in never-never land, last Friday afternoon, decided to put this stock and I randomly got selected to take 1,000 shares of this stock. Now, if this stock opened up at $80 a share rather than $96 a share, I could have lost big time.

Now, I hear you asking, well what is my safety protection then? I mean, if I go into the close and I think that I am okay, is there really any safety, because could the stock tank after the market closes and then I may get this stock put to me without even knowing about it? It is as if you are watching a basketball game and it came up to the very end of the game and the score was tied and they cleared everybody out of the building and they played overtime in secret. Well, that doesn't happen in basketball, but it looks like it happens in the stock market. This overtime was played in secret and it could sneak up on any one of us and catch us off-guard, especially if the stock were to tank.

So here is my strategy of warning and recommendation, which is to clean house to monitor your accounts better. If you are worried about a position, (such as a covered call position, a bull call spread or a sold put position) being exercised on and you are above the strike price in a put position or below the strike price in a covered call position, you may want to, right up to the expiration time, even a few days before, clean house. This means that you could buy back the put that you sold for even $\frac{1}{16}$ or possibly even $\frac{1}{8}$. It may behoove you to do so. Why would you want to stay in an obligation position even after the market closes when the stock is close to the strike price? You would have the risk of the stock put to you or having a stock called away from you that you don't want to have called it away from you.

So, to reiterate, if one or two days before an expiration date you can close out your position, either by buying back the sold call position or by buying back the sold put position, it may be a good idea to do so. You would 1) free up margin, for even those few days, and 2) you would end the obligation to perform, which obligation could get you in trouble if you leave this position open after the market closes on Friday afternoon.

This is the type of trade we put on W.I.N.™ all the time. W.I.N.™ is a great resource wherein real I post trades for my subscribers to read. It's great tutorial information because you can look over the shoulder of people who trade and make money in the stock market every day. You'll see trades not only from me, but also from my Team Wall Street instructors.

If you call now and mention this book, I'll make you a special introductory offer–five days of W.I.N.™ for only $10. That's five days full of trades, plus access to our great research sections and the journal of trades, which shows you what we've been doing for the last few months. Don't miss out. Call 1-800-872-7411 today.

SUMMARY

Monthly returns of 20, 40, and 60%. Figure out your risk and profits in advance. Steady income now. The ability to undo and redo the position. Very low cash (hold) involved and a strategy brokers love (once they learn it) and will let you do, plus option market makers enjoy. Tell me, what gets steadier than this?

Practice, ponder, and practice.

**The great thing in this world
is not so much where we are, but in
what direction we are moving.**

Oliver Wendell Holmes

CHAPTER 12

BEAR PUT, BEAR CALL, AND CALENDAR SPREADS

My second favorite spread is the bear call spread. It is a credit spread. Need I say more? We'll get to the bear call spread shortly, but I want to make a few general comments and cover the bear put spread first. We'll spend ample time on bear call spreads after that.

There are four basic types of spreads: the bull call spread (BUCS), the bull put spread (BUPS), the bear call spreads (BECS), and the bear put spreads (BEPS). And there are many variations on the theme. There are nifty ways to get in, get a better fill, and undo the spreads. These creative ways abound. That is not my point in telling you this. My point is that some ways are better than others, and if you're a liberal bent and can't stand being judgmental, let's say that there is a time for everything. There are situations when one spread is more applicable than another or better used.

That's the key, fitting the strategy to the opportunity. Don't use a wrench when you need pliers. I'll begin to sound like a broken record if I say this too many more times, but the stock market (and any particular stock) is going up, going down, or going sideways. Then would it not be nice if there was a strategy that works best in each one of these three situations? Part of this process is simple. In option trading, when a stock is low, sell a put, buy a call; when high (and coming down) sell a call and buy a put. Tandem plays. Two plays up, two plays down. Add stock purchases, pure stock buys, sells, and spreads, and you have several plays up, several plays down.

I'm amazed when I hear commentators on TV and radio say, "You can make money in any market." Oh yea, show me I say, and very few have answers and fewer yet have ever really done so. Tell me, show me, and prove it. It's tough and even though the formulas exist, few really know how. Obviously its easier to make money when the market is going up, but you know, the market or a particular stock can sure pull back quickly. It may take weeks for a stock to get from $60 to $70, but it can pull back to $62 in seconds with even good news, or unfounded rumors or bad news.

Coming up I'll show you two plays, spreads to be exact, for downturns, peaks, new highs, or any type of a downtrending market or stock. The first one, a bear put spread is a debit spread. I'm not too fond of this one so we won't spend much time on it.

Bear Put Spread

In a sell put situation we purchased the underlying option position for protection, to eliminate some risk, and to limit our margin requirement. We sold the overriding put for income. Selling the put was also the action that required our commitment to perform. We do bull put spreads when the stock is low and going up. In a bear put spread the stock is high and coming down.

The stock has run up from $74 to $82. You think it's coming down. Look at the numbers.

The $75 put is 50¢ x 75¢

The $80 put is $3.25 x $3.50

The $85 put is $6 x $6.25

The $90 put is $9.75 x $10

We would sell the $80 put for $3.25 and buy the $85 put for $6.25. In a bear put spread we want the stock to get put to us so we hope the stock goes below $80. We have spent $3, or $3,000 and we'll make $5,000 (minus the $3,000), or a $2,000 profit. I won't explain all the mechanics. Suffice it to say that as the stock goes down, the value of your $85 put goes up. The stock gets put to you, but simultaneously, the $85 put is exercised–you in fact put the stock that just got put to you to the next guy. In short, if it drops you make $2,000. Like the bull call spread, we spend money, so to make the $2,000 we need the option to be exercised. The way that this one works is for the stock to be below $80 so it will get put to us.

Now to be certain the stock is put to us, move up a set of strike prices. Do an $85/$90 put spread. Sell the $85 put and buy the $90. Here we go:

Buy the $90 put for $10,000

Sell the $85 put for $6,000

You have $4,000 invested. If the stock stays below $85, it all works well. You make $1,000 on a $4,000 investment or 25%. One thousand dollars is not as much as the $2,000 for the $80/$85 put, but there is less risk.

You use this strategy when the stock hits a peak and starts to pull back. The problem once again is that second set of commissions. Upon expiration, you have two positions to exercise. Review the commentary on bull call spreads. In short, a bear put spread is a debit spread. Debit spreads have an entering set of commissions, and an exit set of commissions. So again, unless you get a really good commission arrangement (like zero on the exercise) then why do it? The commissions, if you have four of them, will eat up a large part of the profit. In the last example of a $1,000 profit, the commission could be $400 to $600. Let's look at the bear call spread.

BEAR CALL SPREAD

This is my second favorite type of spread. Again, you use bear spreads when you think a stock has spiked up and will come down or is in a type of down market, even a downward drifting market or stock. Let's use the same example. The stock has gone up from $74 to $82. It's on the way down, or on a pullback.

The call numbers are as follows:

The $80 call is $4 x $4.25

The $85 call is $2 x $2.25

The $90 call is $1 x $1.25

Let's do it! We sell the $85 call and buy the $90 call. By selling the $85 call, we're agreeing to sell or deliver the stock at $85. Fat chance as the stock is pulling back. Here's what we make:

Sell the $85 call for $2

Buy the $90 call for $1.25

We take in $2,000 and spend $1,250. We pocket $750. This is a credit spread. That $750 is in our account the next day. The hold in our account is the spread of $5,000 less the $750 of cash generated from the sale, or $4,250.

Let's see what happens. The stock drops from $82 to $78 or so. There is no way at this price that it will get called away. On the expiration day, all options expire worthless. We keep the $750; $750 on $4,250 (hold) is about an 18% return. There is no second set of commissions as there is no exercising of the options.

If the stock rises, we could lose the $4,250 but long before that, we would buy back the position and maybe roll up to the next strike prices, like the $90 call (sell) and the $95 call (buy).

When it works right, you'll wonder why you purchased the $90 call. It was just insurance, but it also limited our risk, and this makes the play safer so our brokers will let us do the spread. The spread limited our margin. At this writing, I can't think of one bear call spread where we lost money. Now, as of late, the market has been very bullish, so we don't use this type of spread much. In the summer of 1998, the market downtrended and we put in place many bear call spreads.

There is a time and a place for every spread. Let's look at a high flyer. The premiums will seem outrageous. A hi-tech company has run up from $80 to $110. A stock split was announced and it spiked up to $124. The numbers:

The $120 call is $8 x $8.25

The $125 call is $6 x $6.25

The $130 call is $3.75 x $4

The $135 call is $2 x $2.25

We could do the $125/$130 spread or we could do the $130/$135 spread. We could also do the $125/$135, a $10 spread.

Let's look at the $125/$130 spread first. Question: Do we want to get called out or not? Let's see. We sell the $125 call for $6, or $6,000. We buy the $130 protection call for $4, or $4,000. We would net $2,000 profit.

$6,000 income
(-)$4,000 expenses
$2,000 net credit into our account

If we shop, we could get $2,250 or a little more. We put $2,000 cash in our account. This will be a 60% return on our investment (again, it's money on hold, or $3,000). Why so much profit? Because the $124 is so close to the $125 strike price. There is a likelihood we'll get called out–all the stock has to do is move up a few points.

So, for a safer deal, let's move up a strike price, sell the $130 call for $3.75 or $3,750 and buy the $135 call for $2.25 or $2,250.

$3,750 income
(-)$2,250 expenses
$1,500 net credit into our account

It's less cash but more protection. You see the stock has to rise above $130 now for things to turn bad. And it just might. It is coming up on a split, and with other good news, it could easily rise. Again, we do this on stocks that are coming down.

So let's move up again. The $140 call is 75¢ x $1. Let's sell the $135 call for $2, or $2,000 and spend $1,000 to buy the $140 call. We pocket $1,000 profit on a $4,000 hold in our account. Now the stock would have to move up $11 more in the next few weeks. If it does move up there is still time to wind out, et cetera. This looks like a good play. It's not as good as a 60% return, but there is a lot more safety. Remember safety is paramount.

We use bear call spreads when we think a stock is coming down, or at least won't go up to the targeted strike price. And think, $1,000 on a $4,000 hold is a 25% one-month return.

> *Note: I will put in place bear call spreads on stock going through a stock split after a rally into the ex-dividend date, or shortly thereafter. There is just too much momentum if the stock is in the early stages of the split process. We're looking for a downswing, not a stock moving up. We want the options to expire in a bear call spread.*

Bear call spreads are like bull put spreads in that they only have one set of commissions if the spread works right. To further summarize, I use my two favorite spreads for up and down movements in the stock. The bull put spread is used when the stock is going up. The bear call spread is used when the stock is going down.

CALENDAR SPREAD

Let's change gears and do an add-on strategy. If we own an option on a particular stock we can sell calls against that position. The sell position could be at a higher strike price for the same month, and at a higher strike price, or even the same strike price for a different month, or closer expiration date. We sell calls to generate income. This income can be used to offset the cost of buying the further out calls.

Let's see this last one at work. You like a stock. It's going to $80. You buy the $100 call out six months for $12. You could now write the next month out $100 calls for, say $2, or $2,000. That's a nice credit, and cash in our account. We have just lowered our $12,000 option cost basis to $10,000. If the stock stays below $100, we will not get called out. We still own the position and next month sell the $100 call for $2.25 once again. The stock has even moved up to $88. That's $2,250 more income. We can do this month after month.

A few tips. We don't want to get called out in this strategy until we are very profitable. We just want to keep generating income on a leveraged, or option position. So my idea is to sell the short-term option way out of the money. We would lose if we were called out. Let's explore what you might be tempted to do. Again, we've spent $12,000 and purchased 10 contracts of the, say December options. It's now July. The near-term options for August look like this:

The $80 call is $8

The $85 call is $6

The $90 call is $4

The $95 call is $3

The $100 call is $2

Wow, we see the $85 calls at $6 or $6,000. That's great income. But if the stock moves up to $85 or above, you'll get called out. In theory, you'd have to exercise your $100 call options to deliver the stock and you would lose your $12,000 option premium. If the stock stays below $85, you're okay. My point is that you need to be careful. That's why I try to sell the near term options for the same strike price as the further out position. If not the $100 calls, then maybe the $95 calls.

And, and, and I do those way out there.

Let's look at this sell once again. If you sell the August $90 call and you own the December $100 call, you have backed into a bear call spread. In a BECS, you don't want to get called out. You want the stock to go down, stay down, or at least not go up.

LEAPS®

Many people own LEAPS®. LEAPS® calls are out there for the next two years. They also expire on the third Friday of a January one and two years away. They cost a lot of money because you're buying a lot of time. The sheer expense of LEAPS® has people looking for a way to generate income to offset their high cost.

Okay, generating income is fine, but let's not get carried away. If we pay $26 for a $100 call on a hi-tech popular stock, it would cost $26,000 for 10 contracts. It's not that high when you think of the time left and the 1,000 shares you control at the $100 price.

The next month out $100 calls are going for just $1. The $1,000 of income is tempting and probably, with your luck you'd sell the option for the $1,000 and within two weeks, the stock is at $102 and you lose $25,000. That's the $26,000 premium expense minus the $1,000 income.

So, here are a few thoughts.

1. Write calls against stocks you want to sell–do it for the income.

2. Write calls against options at a close strike price–a bull call spread–for the same month.

3. Write calls against options at nearer term dates, but at the same strike price, or close to the same price. You don't want to get exercised on.

SUMMARY OF THE FOUR BASIC SPREADS

Bull Call Spread
- Use in uptrend.
- Use when stock is going up.
- Debit spreads, cash flow 18 to 25% per month.
- Possible extra commission when exercised on.

Bull Put Spread
- Use in uptrend in stock, or on dip.
- The options expire–no extra commissions.
- Limits risk; limits margin.
- In use by me a lot because when the market is good these can produce as much as 20 to 60% monthly returns.

Bear Put Spread
- Use in downtrend; may require four commissions; limits exposure and risk.
- Debit spreads cost money to put in place (this amount is the hold amount).

Bear Call Spread

- Use for downtrending stock, or after a stock has peaked.

- Credit spreads—income generator; limited risk, hold or margin amount is lessened.

- Upon expiration, they expire—no second set of commissions

All Of Them

- Can be unwound and undone if the stock or options move wrong. You can buy back and move up or down. They are all doable. You'll need to find a stockbroker who knows how to do these spreads—one with a lot of experience.

Note: For more information on my Spread and Butter Seminar call 1-800-872-7411.

Life has taught me to expect nothing,
but she has to expect success to be
the inevitable result of my endeavors.
She taught me to seek sustenance
from the endeavor itself, but to leave
the result to God.

Alan Paton

CHAPTER 13

INDEX PLAYS AND INDEX SPREADS

Options are interesting animals. They are a security which is derived from or based on an underlying security, hence the name derivative. There are basically four types of options: Stock Options, Interest Rate Options, Foreign Currency Options, and Index Options.

There is a never-ending quest to "bet right" or guess right the movement of the options. Fortunes can be made or lost in minutes or hours. This quest has at its heart and soul the study of the relationship between the underlying security and the derivative. The formulas for equating the two could fill up two or three pages in a book. I don't even pretend I want my life to get that complicated.

I use simple charts, or just follow the numbers mentally to judge my entrance and exit point. I also think all four option arenas are learnable and playable by the average American once he or she has studied them, practiced them and goes through the learning curve. This section will deal with particular stock indices. I feel strongly that for safety investing, indices and spiders (SPDRS) are a good diversification strategy.

Let's ponder stock movements. What causes a stock to go up or down? Is it the market as a whole? Are movements caused by things going on in a particular sector or industry, or is it news about that specific stock?

It doesn't take a detailed or extensive examination to realize the broader movements usually control a particular stock's movement. A stock may have awesome news, but the whole market is down–it's hard for it to buck the trend. A whole sector rises with a few good earnings announcements and even lesser known stocks or stocks which aren't doing so well rise also. At least we see that earnings report, either good or bad, affects a company's neighboring competitor's stocks.

Someone has surmised that upwards of 70% of a stock's movement is caused by the market in general–that's the overall market. Around 20% is caused by the sector or industry the stock is in–say all the oil stocks, or the bank stocks, et cetera. Only around 10% of a movement is caused by the stock itself. From my observations I don't think this is too far off. Now review the numbers: 70%, 20%, and 10%. If it's true then why aren't we playing the bigger picture?

Indices allow us to do just that. An index is a group of stocks, and by using some mathematical formula, a price or value is set for this group. You can use small sector indices like the Japan Index–or Euro index. There is a hi-tech index and recently a new one was created with just Internet stocks. There are indices that cover hundreds of companies like the SPX–this one is for all the Standard & Poors 500 companies. (There is a new one which started trading in mid March, 1999–it is based upon the NASDAQ 100 stocks and the ticker symbol is QQQ.) The OEX is the largest 100 stocks in the Standard & Poors. The OEX is my favorite, because it is widely traded.

These indices are different than mutual funds. Indices don't own stocks. There are no management fees. Indices are made up. They are contrived to chart bigger movements. We can buy derivatives on these contrivaties.

ROLLING MARKETS

I love stocks that roll. We get in, get out, and make money. They are predictable to a certain extent. Well guess what? Sometimes the whole market is on a roll. Look at the following charts.

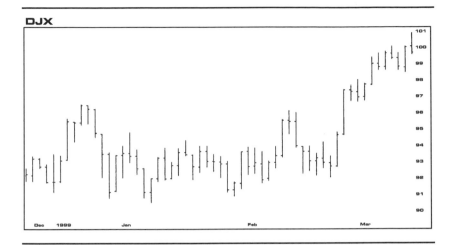

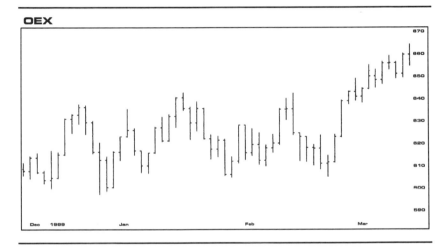

Look at how many times you could get in and get out. These indices to an extent are more certain than a single stock. There's safety in numbers.

AMERICAN VS. EUROPEAN STYLE OPTIONS

Options are what you play on indices. If the OEX is at 642 you could buy the 630, 635, or 640 or even $650 call options. You can also buy put options if you think the index is going down. Some indices have $1 strike prices. Most indices are European style.

American style options are options that can be exercised any time up to and including the expiration date.

European style options can only be exercised on their expiration date. Up until now in all my option discussions we have only dealt with the American style ones. That's because stock options in the United States are all American style. However, most indices in the United States use European style trading. One other thing, these index investments settle for cash. You see, there is no stock purchase. You own a position on the index. Let's say you buy the OEX 640 for $12 and the OEX goes to 660. On expiration date (the next day) you will have $20 in your account.

If you lose and the OEX goes to 630 then $10 is taken out of your account. Please note: these options are like other options in some ways. The premium is made up of intrinsic value and time value. You can buy an index in the money. The OEX is at 642. You could buy the 630 calls or the 620. You can buy out of the money calls like the 650 or 660 if you think the OEX is going up.

The time value erodes just like a stock option. In the above example we could have made more and lost less by selling at a better time than the expiration date. Now, you ask, "I thought you just said they could only be exercised on the expiration." That's correct. But I didn't say buy and sell. We could buy a call at 10:00 AM for $12 and with a rise in the index, the option goes to $15 by 1:00 PM, and we sell, pocketing the $3. Now, index options are in 100 unit contracts. One contract at $12 will be $1,200, 10 contracts is $12,000. We control 100, or 1,000 positions at that price. This number of 100 is called the index multiplier.

THE DOW

For many years the Dow or the DJIA would not let indices use their stocks in this manner, but a few years ago they loosened the reins. Now there are indices representing certain sectors of the Dow kingdom. DJIA, the 30 industrials or DJX. This index is $\frac{1}{100}$ of the DJIA (0.01). If the Dow is at 9,650 then the index is 96.50. Strike prices are in one-dollar intervals. The transportation sector of the Dow has its own index: the transportation index or DTX. This index is $\frac{1}{10}$ of the transports (0.10). If the transports are at 3,230, then the

DTX is 323. It trades in $5 increments for the strike prices. Utilities, the index of utility companies, or the DUX is at the same price. If the utilities are at 329 then the index is 329. It is in $5 increment strike prices.

Look at these charts:

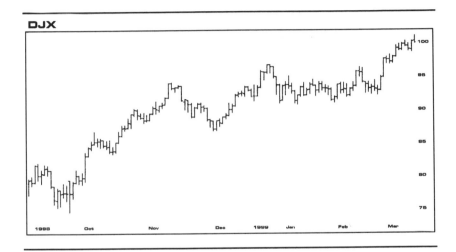

Here are some other indices.

NAME	SYMBOL	STYLE
Biotechnology	BTK	European
Computer Technology	XCI	American
Dow Jones Industrials	DJX	European
Gold/Silver	XAU	American
Institutional	XII	European
Internet	IIX	European
Japan	JPN	European
NASDAQ 100	NDX	European
NYSE Composite	NYA	European
Pharmaceutical	DRG	European
S&P 100	OEX	American
S&P 500	SPX	European
S&P Small Cap 600	SML	European
Value Line	VLE	European

These smaller indices should not be ignored, but only used when you understand the components, chart the movements, and practice trading on them. I've made a lot of money on the DJX. However, remember we're after all the safety we can get. If we think there is safety in broader indices or broader plays then look at the SPX and then the OEX. The SPX is a great grouping of companies. Look at the roll patterns; look at the mountain peaks and valleys. Are you formulating how to play any of these opportunities?

I read a report that talked about the value of the truly large companies on the S&P 500. It was something like this: 37 companies made up 53% of the market-capitalized value on the S&P 500. You see the true wealth is in a small group of huge companies. To get a narrow based group—say these 37 plus a few more larger companies, then go for the S&P 100, or the OEX.

THE OPTION PREMIUM

The amount of money you will spend for index options will seem quite expensive, but remember what you're buying. If the index follows a rather volatile batch of stocks, there will be the same high premiums as a single volatile stock. For example the premiums of IIX, an Internet index, are extremely expensive. And with this expensive risk goes the chance of making big profits. You can lose quickly too. This index only covers a dozen or so stocks. That is a pretty narrow focus.

Even the OEX has big swings. The options are not cheap. Also let me implant in your brain a fairly good comparison between the OEX and the DJIA (Dow 30). The Dow Jones 30 industries are the most widely watched group in the world. We think when we hear the Dow is up 70 or down 30 that the world market has moved the same way. Nothing could be further from the truth. The point for this discussion is that we hear it all the time, we mentally monitor the Dow.

There is a loose comparison or ratio between the Dow and the OEX, and it is one to 16. A 16 point movement on the Dow translates to about a one point move on the OEX.

Let's see what this means in real life. The Dow runs up to 11,120 the OEX is at 695. You think it has peaked out. You buy a

670 put. For the OEX to drop 5 points the Dow will have to go down around 80 points. The Dow can do that in a heartbeat. We don't need the OEX to drop to 670 to make money. Remember, we get magnified movements in our options.

Let's say the Dow pulls back to 10,720 the OEX is down to 670. For the OEX to go from 670 to 680, or 10 points, it would translate into about a 160 point move in the Dow. I hope you're seeing opportunities here. Look at the prices.

OEX:

The 670 calls are $18

The 680 calls are $14

The 690 calls are $10

The 700 calls are $8

Let's buy 10 contracts of the 690 calls for $10 or $10,000. We need a 300 point move for maximum profitability. But even if the DOW only moves up 100 points the OEX moves up 7 or 8 points and the 690 calls are now $16, we sell for a $6,000 profit.

We do index options, like options on stocks, in many circumstances. We should do our homework. We definitely should chart these movements. We should know our exit points–either a percentage, a set profit we're happy with, or whatever. These are not meant to be long-term trades, but short term: day or week trades. Remember the "meter drop."

IN THE MONEY

If we think the whole market is down we can buy in the money, at or close to the money, or out-of-the-money calls. Let's say the OEX drops to 660. That's way down. For days it bounces around here. A few good earnings reports come out (remember there are only 100 stocks that make up this index) and the group index starts to move up.

The 650 calls are $21

The 660 calls are $16

The 670 calls are $9

The 680 calls are $5

We will probably get a bigger bang for our buck by buying the 670 or 680 calls. Remember a 10 point move would correspond to a 160 point move in the Dow. For more safety we could buy the 650 strike price, in-the-money calls. Of the $21 option premium $10 is intrinsic value, or in the money, $11 is the time value in the premium. As the stock moves up, the option on a corresponding ratio moves up–magnified. Watch:

INDEX	650 CALL OPTION
660	$21
664	$23
668	$26
672	$29

A 12 point move in the Index (a 192 point move in the Dow: 16 x 12 points = 192) has our option increasing to $29; $21,000, becomes $29,000 in hours or days. That's an $8,000 profit. Hit the movies and do another one tomorrow.

If the OEX goes down, and the option premium decreases we could sell at a loss or wait for a turnaround. That's up to you and your broker.

SPREADS

With this $21 option purchased, we could now sell the 680 calls (or the 690 or 700) for $5,000 at the current time. What would that mean? We take in $5,000 and now agree to sell the index option at 680. If the index goes up, but doesn't get to 680 we won't be called out. The 680 option expires and we keep the $5,000. Another way to look at this is that we've lessened the cost of the 650 calls we purchased. We are long the 650 calls, but short the 680 calls. That's a $30 profit (spread) we've created at a cost of $16. To maximize the profits we would have to get called out at 680. However we don't think, or necessarily need that to happen. If the index goes to 675 or so, we can sell the 650 calls and buy back the 680 calls.

Margin requirements on index options are treated just like stocks. If you sell a naked call at 680 for $5,000 you'll need to have about $20,000 to $25,000 on hold; 680 would translate to $68,000 (for 10 contracts). However if you own the 650 call, it creates a spread. Margin is your net cost, or $16,000. The potential exists to make $14,000 on a $16,000 hold. It probably won't happen.

The eroding premium becomes a factor. Yes, the index is going up. The time value of the 650 calls starts to go away. Remember part of the value of the option is the time. As we get closer to the expiration date the fluff (time value) will start to deteriorate in both the 650 call and the 680 call. If the index got to say, 674 the week of expiration, the 650 could be going for $26 and the 680 strike price for $2 or so. We could buy back the 680 call for $2,000 (we net $3,000—we sold it for $5,000) The 650 call we purchased for $21 is now $26, another $4, or $4,000 profit. A week ago the 650 call was at $31, we should have sold it back then—even if we had to pay $4 to $6 to buy back the 680 call.

Practice trading these, or do Simutrades™. Track prices so you can get a feel for:

1. The index swings and corresponding option price swings.

2. Relationships between the Dow (DJIA), the OEX, and the corresponding options.

3. The time value of the premium. How time becomes your enemy (especially for high-valued options).

Now that you've seen a spread created—actually we backed into this one—can we not intentionally set up a spread? Yes, and all four types of spreads can be worked. My favorite is the bull put spread so let's just do that one. Why not do the others? Here's why. Why not get down one formula and apply it everywhere?

I've written on bull put spreads extensively in another chapter. You should read that first, and maybe several times before you read this next part. You must understand the mechanics of bull put spreads to understand the following. Index options are expensive so they present opportunities to make a lot of money. Think it through to "Z." If the premiums are expensive to buy, why not be a seller, not a buyer.

Let's keep using the same examples. The OEX is way down to 660. It has fallen 30 points–about a 400+ point drop in the Dow. All indications are that this is the bottom. Here are the put prices:

STRIKE PRICE	COST
630	$6
640	$9
650	$15
660	$19
670	$22
680	$29

If we sell the 640 puts (naked) for $9, or $9,000, the index would have to drop another 20 points for us to get in trouble. Our margin will be about $18,000 (that's about 25 to 30% of $64,000) (see the premium hold and margin requirements in the chapter Selling Puts for Income Generation). Since we are talking about a cash settled index, your brokerage firm will treat the 640 strike price as $64. Take that for 10 contracts, which controls 1,000 units (1 contract controls 100 units, therefore 10 contracts x 100 units = 1,000) x $64 or $64,000. A $9,000 profit on a $18,000 hold for one month is a nice return. No, it's a great return! Since this is a naked put, your broker may not let you sell these no matter how much money you have in your account.

So, let's sell the 650 puts for $15, or $15,000 and buy the 640 for $9, or $9,000. That's $15,000 income and $9,000 expense. That means we have a credit of $6,000. Since we are setting up a $10 spread, our margin requirement is $4,000. That is:

Spread X number of units: $10 X 1,000 = $10,000
Minus amount of credit $6,000
Equals the amount of margin required: $4,000

We net $6,000 on a $4,000 investment or a return of 150%!

Happy days are here again. A $6,000 gain on a $4,000 require-ment. And think, the OEX would have to drop another 20 points (or 320+ points on the Dow). We did our homework and the Dow and OEX were going back up. If they do drop we can still buy back our position. The $4,000 margin requirement is the most we could lose if the OEX falls down. But we could buy back the 650 option we sold and sell now, or later, the 640 put we own.

If the index goes up we could just let the spread positions expire, or we could end our obligation by winding out. Let's explore this. The OEX goes up to 680 just like we expected. The options are now going for the following.

PUT OPTION	OPTION PRICE
640	$2
650	$5
660	$9
670	$14
680	$20
690	$26
700	$34

We wind out or end the position. Buy back the 650 puts for $5,000 and sell the 640 puts for $2. This makes us break-even. Spend $5,000, take in $2,000 = $3,000 to unwind. We originally took in $3,000. So it might be best to just wait it out until the expiration. If the OEX moves up more and we can get out at a cost of say $1,000 maybe it would be worth it. We would net $2,000 and our obligation is over. If the OEX hits 680 and you think it is still going up you could end the last spread and do a 650/660 put spread or the 670/680 spread. Sell the 680 for $20,000, and buy the 670 for $14,000. That's a net of $6,000. The hold is $10,000 minus the $6,000, or $4,000. That's over a 100% return, but the risk is much greater. The OEX can definitely drop below 680, and very quickly. The greater the risk the greater the profit potential. But why risk it?

Conclusion

In short, I do bull puts spreads on the OEX index, but way out of the money. Usually I choose a strike price 30 to 40 points below the current level of the OEX, or a corresponding index. Remember, safety first with nice steady cash flow–$20,000 will generate about $4,000 to $8,000 per month on these safer, way out-of-the-money bull put spreads.

Not to be able to bear poverty is a shameful thing; but not to know how to chase it away by work is a more shameful thing yet.

Pericles

CHAPTER 14

THE BEST FORMULA

As always, I save the best for last. I often think, as I get in front of an audience, what I could possibly say that will help them, truly help them do things better—and *be* better. I have the same question now. What can I possibly write that will make a substantial difference in your life?

First let me thank you for sticking with this book up to this point. I started in the Preface with the thought of explaining holistic cash flow investing. We need our money to have more personality. It needs to work harder. If we cannot achieve this, then we have to keep working too hard. If we can get our money working with more personality then we can find ourselves doing the truly important things in life.

I often ask, "Could you be a little bit better you if you had more money coming in?" Most attendees nod yes. Money will not make you good or bad, it will only speed you along the road you're already on a little faster. If you're a good person, money will make you a better person. If you're a bad person; whining, bad attitude, cross; then money will make you worse.

It is to help you be on the road to good living—even great living—that I address these final remarks. My books *Business Buy the Bible*,

A+ (my current favorite), and *Don't Set Goals* address many of these situations far more extensively than I will do here. But there are a few principles that I'd like to leave with you.

The principle of giving is not only a spiritual, but also a financial principle. Giving transcends boundaries. I get such a thrill out of the hundreds, indeed, thousand of letters and comments from people who are giving more and feeling such wonderful feelings. I'll share with you two letters; one to me from a boy named Zeve; one to Zeve from the LA Mission.

"Dear Mr. Cook,

My name is Zeve Akerling, and I'm twelve. Thanks to your rolling stocks strategy, I made my first (and successful) trade, on Madge Networks, (MADGF). I bought at six and a quarter and sold around seven. I made about $160 after commission and I'm waiting for it to come back down to six again.

I have read all of your books, and I agree with your opinion about tithing, and plan to do so after each successful trade. Do you have a favorite charity where you send your donations?

I hope to be going to the movies a whole lot more often using your strategies!

> Yours truly,
> Zeve Akerling"

"Dear Zeve Akerling:

Thank you so very much for your gift of $16.00 in honor of Mr. Wade B. Cook.

Your gift allows us to help homeless men and women by providing them with food, shelter, clothing, love, compassion and a listening ear.

Many homeless people we serve have given up hope for the future...they are hungry, not only for food, but for love.

Because of your help, we are here 24 hours a day to tell them there is hope...that there are people who care.

Thank you again for your compassion for those in need.

With God's Blessing

> Mike Edwards, President,
> Los Angeles Mission"

I'll take all the criticism in the world to help one young boy "get it." My wife's Uncle Bob is a gem of a person. In fact, I dedicated my book *Y2K Gold Rush* to him because he is pure gold. He said one time, "You throw your bread on the water and it comes back buttered." I hope God in His eternal wisdom will one day share with me how the principle of giving works.

I know it does, I see it all around me. Some say "Well it's easy for you to give, you have much." I say, "Don't wait to be generous, be generous and wait." Remember the widow's mite.

Is the sum total of our investing to make more, to be "rich," or is it to do good–to make a genuine impact? *Safety 1st Investing* was written to help us build and preserve assets that produce income. However, our most precious asset is our relationship with God. We need to take spiritual vitamin pills every day. We need to work at this relationship more seriously than the stock market. It produces bigger dividends.

I read recently about the difference between a good manager and a good leader. A good manager, so it goes, is a person who does things the right way. A leader is one who does the right things. Most of us spend way too much time doing things the right way, and though this is very important, it is vital we find ourselves doing the right things. With God it's the same. He speaks of prospering, sharing, one-hundred-fold returns, wealth; and he asks so little. He wants us to walk in His covenant. That is the right thing.

The wealth, the blessings will come according to Eternal Providence. We work to make it happen, but we will find great satisfaction, great strength, and great happiness doing the right things. The truly right things.

I started this book writing of formulas. There are formulas everywhere. Formulas for prosperity, formulas for failure; formulas for a life of achievement, a life of happiness; and formulas for the opposite. There are formulas of the world, and formulas of God.

In my small way I've tried to show, to teach of these financial formulas. Why? So many people who gain an understanding of these wealth formulas will learn the process, and do the works.

Practice these trades. I hope gaining this knowledge will help you do more and be more, and know the principle of working a formula. Then, hopefully someday you will want a truly full life, a life of meaning, compassion, and understanding. Then you will seek out the formulas that will help achieve this. You'll know the power of observation. You'll experience the results of learning and applying what you've learned. You'll know the magic of "sticking to the recipe." You'll know how to make things happen. You'll be better able to make things happen for God.

APPENDIX 1

IS THE STOCK MARKET FOR YOU?

Some time ago I walked into the daily sales meeting and asked each and every person there to write a letter explaining the Wall Street Workshop™ and why someone like you should attend. Then I asked our speakers at the bimonthly speaker training to do the same. These letters were to be explicit, exciting, include testimonials, and contain personal experiences. You see, what I want you to understand is that many of our best salespeople and speakers were first students just like you. They came through a Wall Street Workshop™, learned the formulas and strategies, and became very successful. And like me, they wanted to share this knowledge with everyone they could, so they came to work here or joined Team Wall Street to be on the road teaching.

There is something magical and exciting about finally becoming aware that you have the knowledge, skill, and confidence to take control of your financial future. You want to share it with family and friends so they too can partake of this knowledge. I would venture to say that a lot of you have bought this book because a friend or family member told you about it. Deep down we all want the best for our family and ourselves. I get a little emotional when I think about all the people who have changed their lives because of what they were able to learn at the Wall Street Workshop™.

Once the letters were written I had my staff collect them and select the best parts from many of them to include in this appendix. So for the next few pages you will be shown how attending the Wall Street Workshop™ can change your life. Remember, these stories and testimonials you are about to read are about or from actual students who took the first steps toward changing how they live by experiencing the Wall Street Workshop™. Now these are some extraordinary stories and not everybody may achieve to this degree. But what you need to know is that every one of these people started right where you are, as a beginner with the Wall Street Workshop™ strategies. It is up to you how far you go with them.

I'm sure you are asking yourself, "Why do I need to learn this from Wade Cook Seminars? Do these strategies really work?" It's not very often that the information companies or individuals use to make millions of dollars becomes common knowledge. Typically, companies keep secret designs, formulas, recipes, and ideas under lock and key. That way they are in control. For many years, the stock market was only for the rich and powerful. These people were the only ones with the secrets. Years ago I opened those locks and discovered that there are no real mysteries to the stock market. You just need to know the rules and how to play. I learned the rules through trial and error, planning trades, trying new formulas, challenging the "good ol' boys" and winning. After several years of perfecting these methods, and a focus on eliminating as much risk as possible through careful research and common sense, the Wall Street Workshop™ was born. This seminar was developed to teach hard-hitting, time-tested, proven formulas and strategies. Each strategy when applied correctly can generate unbelievable returns on your investments.

There are two things that keep people from making money in the market: fear and lack of knowledge. The Wall Street Workshop™ teaches you how to overcome both. Once you have the knowledge of what to do and how to play, fear is replaced by confidence, and once this happens there are no limitations to your success. When you learn these strategies you are putting yourself in control. You are taking control and responsibility for your future. You are no longer leaving your money in the hands of your broker. Do you think your broker cares about your money like you do? No one, and I mean no one, will manage your money with your best interest in mind except you. This reminds me of an experience that Doug Sutton, one of our Team Wall Street instructors, wrote about in his letter. Here is what Doug had to say:

"This story is about Bill, a stockbroker who attended my Wall Street Workshop™ in Cleveland last summer. It is special to me because we don't get a lot of brokers attending our seminars and of those who do, most just seem to be interested in trying to sign up prospective clients. Bill was different, however. He was there to learn something new.

I made a comment early in Day One that when the students leave the seminar after two days they will have more knowledge than 90% of the brokers who handle their accounts. The afternoon of the second day Bill approached me and said how much he was learning and how true my statement was about the lack of brokers' knowledge.

Later that fall I was teaching a Workshop in Indianapolis, I think, and there was Bill doing a retake. We spoke for a while and he shared how the Wall Street Workshop™ had changed his life and that of many of his clients. Since taking the Workshop he had a renewed interest in his profession. He said that he found himself wanting to get up early in the morning to prepare for the market. That he was looking at it differently and by employing the strategies we taught there he had made more money for himself and his clients than he had ever done previously."

Now let's see what another broker who wrote to us had to say:

"I am writing to you to let you know that there is one more broker that is completely sold on your strategies. The Wall Street Workshop™ was more than I expected. I went to the Boston Workshop last week. If I could sum it up in one word, it would be explosion! I was really impressed in how your instructors pulled out all the stops and let us have it, so to speak, as far as the detailed formulas. These are literally life changing strategies. I know that I can never look at investing in the same light again.

Thank you for all that you have done for me, as well as my business! You really are for real!!!!!!!!

Kevin Sullivan
Waterville, ME"

Wouldn't it be great if all brokers were like Bill and Kevin? Unfortunately, most are not and are too stubborn to change. Again, the knowledge you will gain at the Wall Street Workshop™ puts you in control of your money. You can make as little as you want or as much as you want. The choice is yours, not someone else's. Isn't the true definition of financial freedom being able to do what you want when you want as long as it is legal? Maybe you want to spend more time with your family, take a vacation, buy a new car, or donate even more to your favorite charity. Whatever financial freedom means to you, here is a way to achieve it.

I want to share a letter that one of our salespeople received about a man who was able to take back control of his life and do what he loves to do: spend time with his family and paint.

"Dear Wade,

I am writing to tell you about Jared of Durham, NC. I helped him arrange to attend the Atlanta Wall Street Workshop™ in early August 1996.

At the time Jared operated a deli cum art gallery called "Anything Goes," where he served breakfast and lunch (no evening meal), and on the walls he hung his paintings (his great passion). He sold his paintings from time to time and his wife worked to make ends meet in support of their two children.

Jared took enough from his savings to pay for the Workshop and open a brokerage account with $15,000. At the beginning of October 1996, Jared called to tell me he had turned his original $15,000 into $70,000 by the end of September. He was so thrilled about his 60-day gains of $55,000! I was truly happy for him. In November (one month later) he called again. This time to report his nest egg had grown by another $20,000 to $90,000!

He informed me he was so grateful that he took half ($45,000) and set it up in an account for his father who had retired a few years previously, but struggled to make ends meet on a paltry pension.

Early in the New Year (1997) he called to let me know he sold the deli and his wife no longer worked outside the home. They both were spending more time at home with their children and he was devoting more time to painting, his first love.

What a nice success story. He was able to improve the lifestyle not only for himself, wife, and children but also for his father. Everyone benefited!

Emery Baldry"

You too can take charge of your future and make right decisions.

I have talked a lot about what attending the Wall Street Workshop™ will allow you to do. Now let me tell you about the seminar. This is not a rah-rah, touchy-feely, hug-your-neighbor, feel-good seminar. This seminar is raw power. The power of learning 13 different strategies for making money in the stock market. You gain knowledge and knowledge is power.

You will learn to develop your style of investing. Whether you are aggressive and like to be in the fight, competing every day, or prefer to be conservative, floating on your back in your pool while your money goes to work, there is a strategy for you. You will be introduced to a style of teaching that is rare in the seminar industry. This is an experiential seminar. What I mean is that our method of teaching is one of "tell, show, and do." First the instructors will tell you, or teach you about the strategies. Then they will show you how to use them. Then they practice the deals live in class, either on paper with a Simutrade™ or in some cases with their own broker and their own account. That's right, they can get a broker on the phone, patch him in over the intercom, and talk the talk with him right in front of you. That's the experiential part of the seminar. Practicing the deals in class.

Everything you have learned to do well you learned through experience. You didn't read a book about driving and then get in your car and take off. First you read the book, then an instructor showed you how, and then you were allowed to do it yourself. That's how we learn, and that's how we teach at the Wall Street Workshop™. The seminars are held during market hours so you can watch the market go up and down, look at charts using Telechart 2000™, research companies, and discuss them right in class.

This method of teaching is the safest and easiest way for you to learn these 13 strategies and start using them to make money. Rodney Ostlund of Tacoma, one of our current students who is also on our sales force, says: "I was surprised to learn that making money in the stock market isn't extremely difficult, just different in how one approaches the ideas of investing and trading. The application of knowledge is so incredible once one has attained that specialized knowledge. I gained that specialized knowledge at the Wall Street Workshop™ and am learning to perfect it as I continue to actively do deals in today's stock market." Once again, it's the education that you get that makes this a seminar you can't afford to miss.

Before I go on to tell you exactly what you will learn in the Wall Street Workshop™, I want to share with you two main rules of trading.

Rule #1:   Always know your exit before you go in the entrance.

Rule #2:   Don't get greedy.

These rules sound easy enough, but the discipline to follow them can be difficult to obtain. You will start practicing them at the Wall Street Workshop™.

At the Wall Street Workshop™ you will learn the stock market vocabulary–how to talk the talk. You will learn market research, trading criteria, technical analysis, and fundamentals. All of these things go hand in hand with the strategies you will be taught. Once you have talked about these topics then you will be introduced to these strategies:

- Building a Great Portfolio: First you need cash flow, then you need to know where to put it safely.
- Rolling Stocks: The first strategy I learned for cash-flowing stocks, still very powerful.
- Options: A way to control and profit from stocks without having to pay market price; increases returns exponentially.
- Stock Splits: One of the most reliable moneymakers ever, and five ways to play it both short and long term.
- Writing Covered Calls: If you already own stock, this could be your very own monthly "money machine."
- Selling Puts: Put money right in your pocket on stocks that are headed up.
- Peaks and Slams: Profiting from exuberance or panic.
- Bargain Hunting–New Issues: What are IPOs and how can you trade them?

- Bargain Hunting–Turnarounds: How to recognize the best stocks with a bad reputation.

- Bargain Hunting–Spin-offs: New stocks with potential.

- Bargain Hunting–Penny Stocks: Like Turnarounds, Penny Stocks are considered a bad neighborhood, but you can find some beautiful and profitable plays here.

- Range Riders: How to get on board for a terrific ride (and how to tell if you've missed it before you get on!).

- Rolling Options: The same principle as rolling stocks, but with greater returns.

- Balancing Strategies: I sometimes call this double or triple-dipping; how to use multiple strategies to make even more on the same play!

We get hundreds of testimonials from students each month telling us about their trades and what they have been doing in the market. Some of the best ones are about what they have been able to do in their life because they attended the Wall Street Workshop™. Things they could never have afforded to do are now in their reach. Here are a few of their stories:

"Today we made $230,079–January 12, 1999. We made it on CMGI. A Tech stock. In fact, on January 11th, we made $47,855, and on January 7th, we made $46,644. We've made $372,725 in just the opening days of this month. That does not mean we have never lost money. Oh Boy!! Have we lost. But we've never lost a dime when we followed the rules as taught at the Wall Street Workshop™. It was only when human nature took over and we got "greedy," that we ever lost anything. It was only when we got careless. Mostly though, we were on the straight and narrow, as the old saying goes.

Joseph Dietrich"

"Another person who has been successful is my younger 23-year old son in law. He was a university student newly married to my daughter and anxious to learn a way to augment his income to support his new little family that included my first darling little granddaughter. He, Jeff, attended a Wall Street Workshop™ but had no money for trading at the time. His father gave him $1,000 and my husband and I added to that. Being the ambitious, self-confident individual that he was, Jeff started trading options with most of his money, totally contrary to what he had been taught in the Wall Street Workshop™. He quickly lost most of his money and had only $500 left. This sobered him considerably and he decided that if he was going to follow his dreams he needed to do things the "Wade Cook way." This time Jeff was trading as he had been taught and in just two months his $500 had grown into $7,000!!!

Bonnie Granger"

"The Wall Street Workshop™ experience has allowed me to have a lifestyle I want and live the way that I want to live with the time I spend working totally up to me. I have no boss but myself. I have no limitations but my own. What a wonderful gift I gave myself when I decided to learn something new and put my money for the classes and my energy behind strategies that were all new. Thank you, Wade, for making all the strategies available and in a language and format I could understand.

Virginia Haas, student"

"Dear Wade,

My name is Bryan Meares and I have to tell you how my life has changed due to your seminars. Last July my granddad bought your book *Wall Street Money Machine* and was excited with joy with what could be done in the stock market. So he challenged me and my cousin to go with him to your seminars. At the time my life seemed worthless to me. After we went to your seminars I started to think of the possibilities of profit in the market. As a result my cousin and I have now become masters in the stock market. I am only 22 and have not finished college, but I am making more money than most professional brokers.

Now I feel that I have found my destiny, making money! As I started to become more involved in the market I shared with my dad, a well-known preacher, the returns I was making on the money my granddad gave me and my cousin to invest. After he saw what I made in the first two months he was constantly encouraging me to stay at it.

As it all turns out, my cousin and I are in the process of getting our investment advisor license and Series 7 license. My granddad tells us that we have the chance of a lifetime and will be years ahead of most brokers. Now our accountant's firm wants us to be the ones to invest all the money for pastor's pension plans.

Wade, I must tell you that you have taken me from the dumps to a millionaire overnight. All of those countless seminars I went to have paid off. I very much enjoyed your staff and their professionalism. I have been to so may of your seminars that they know me well. To all who read this I must tell you that Wade Cook is for real. He is more than just a teaching money machine; he is a man with Biblical convictions and morals. Thank you so much,

> Bryan Meares, student
> (via e-mail)"

"Dallas was 25 years old with a wife and a new little baby. He had been laid off from his job from corporate downsizing. He had $6,000 to his name. He had been reading *Wall Street Money Machine* and from there attended the Financial Clinic in Orlando, FL. He decided to try investing in options using the stock split strategies he learned. In a month he was able to bring $6,000 to $30,000–and that was before he attended the Workshop! Then he went to the Workshop and was able to soar from there. The last I heard he had brought the $30,000 to $60,000 and was very pleased that his wife and he was now able to both stay home and raise their new baby. What would it have cost Dallas if he had not learned and applied Wade's strategies?

> Dyan,
> a customer representative,
> talking about one of her customers"

Where else can you learn in such great detail 13 different money making strategies? For two solid days your instructors will teach you the ins and outs of these strategies. Let's hear from a few of our students what they have been up to once they attended the Wall Street Workshop™:

(E-mail to one of our sales people, Cindy)

"SUBJECT: Hope builders

Cindy:

My wife and I attended the Wall Street Workshop™ in New Orleans October 22 through 24th in 1997. This was probably the worst time for us to get in, being so "green." After an intense three months' ongoing learning curve and some errors on my part I am happy to report our last week's trades. Now we are really getting excited!

AMFM, post split duck, 1/29/98, 4 contracts of the April $35 calls at $2.75; $1100 out. Sold 2/4/98 at $4.625; $1850 in, $750 gain, 68% return in 4 days.

CPQ, post split duck, 2/3/98, 3 contracts of the April $30 calls at $3.25; $975 out. Sold 2/4/98 at $5.50, $1650 in, $675 gain, 69% return in just one day!

Thanks so much Wade and staff, we certainly needed this confidence builder!

Stan and Sue Carver"

(another e-mail)

"SUBJECT: A Student Thanks You

April '97 I attended the Wall Street Workshop™ in Cherry Hill, NJ. I did lots of studying before and after attending class (your book and tapes). I had $10,000 to invest at the time of the class. I followed the advice in the book and tapes and found a broker and opened an account under my business name. W.I.N.™ has been a great help to me. I opened an IRA account with $23,000, bringing my total $$$ to invest to $33,000. I've followed your principles and have made a total of $16,000 profit as of Nov. 30. My in-laws have been very sick recently and I had to choose between working or doing what I had to do for them. Naturally I did what I wanted and had to do. Money has been very tight. Thank God I took your classes and did what I did. The profit I made is paying the bills.

Thank you, Burt Sklaroff"

(and another e-mail)

"SUBJECT: DELL

Well if I learned one thing from the Workshop it was about getting in on stock splits. I have been watching DELL and I thought all signs were go. Yes it was taking a position and standing strong. Yesterday, I bought May $120 calls on DELL at $8½. By doing that I was giving myself some time, even if there was no split and earnings fell shy. DELL is a good company. So I felt I had covered my angles. Well this morning my 120s were at $12¾.

Isn't that around 12,500% annualized? What a kick. While that is good I still must remain emotionless. I just renewed my W.I.N.™ subscription. Keep churnin' and earnin'.

Side note: That Wade Cook is a crazy man, but I like his style. People still look at me like I am a nut. Well, you have got to take some initiative and go for it. I just recently graduated a year ago. I am now a full-time trader. I have taken $100,000 and in two months and ten days made around $36,000. Wade Cook was the start and ya' know I received one of his tapes one day in the mail. I still don't know who sent it or why. Serendipity or what?

Thanks,

Shawn Reed"

This is the power of knowledge. As you can see, once these people were given the knowledge of using proven strategies to make money in the market there is nothing they can't do. They are in control. No more living paycheck to paycheck or worrying about paying the bills. They have created a steady cash flow that allows them the freedom and peace of mind to live their lives how they want.

Now it is decision time. The Wall Street Workshop™ isn't for everyone, but if you are interested in controlling your own life; if you would like to be the one to say how much money you can make and how many or few hours you work to make it; if you have the vision to see the opportunity this type of education has been for others and can be for you–call 1-800-872-7411 right away and register for the next Wall Street Workshop™. Don't spend any more time sitting on the sidelines. Jump into the game and see what you can accomplish. Once you start investing the Wade Cook way the only limits to your success are the ones you put on it!

APPENDIX 2

PROTECTING ASSETS AND ENHANCING CASH FLOW

DIVIDE AND CONQUER

The most effective strategy for protecting assets is to divide and conquer. Make sure that you do not make all of your money in one legal entity, and that you do not hold all your assets in one entity. Basically, there are three different financial Goliaths. One of them is a lawsuit. The second one is income taxes, which can seriously curtail what you're trying to do. The third one is death taxes.

Now, think about these three again: lawsuits, income taxes, and death taxes. If you make all the money you're going to make under your own name, and if all the assets you hold are held under your own name, then you stand pretty vulnerable. Think about that. Can one lawsuit then wipe out everything? Can having one taxable entity which owns everything cause you to be in a higher tax bracket?

The answer to all three financial problems is to split up your assets and make sure that you do not own all of your things in one legal entity. Let's go through all of these in detail. As we go through them, you'll hear a lot about these entities. If you need more information or forms and documents, once again I'll refer you to the available resources at Wade Cook Seminars, Inc. Call for a catalog.

What we're trying to do is to make sure that you have a lot of money set aside for your retirement, and that as you're growing your assets, you grow as rapidly as possible by keeping the chips on your side of the table. If you have one business that has different risks and exposure levels, protect the other business enterprises you have by owning the different businesses or assets in various legal structures.

If I own three rental properties, I wouldn't want to own them in one corporation or one limited partnership. If I bought a Chinese restaurant I would want that in a separate, distinct corporation. If I had a 20-unit apartment building I'd want that in yet a different limited partnership.

This allows for different tax treatment. Each is isolated away from each other. Somebody coming into my Chinese restaurant corporation and suing it would affect that corporation. That corporation may even have to go bankrupt, but it would not affect the other corporations and it would not affect me personally. So again, the theme behind this whole concept is to divide and conquer.

A CORPORATION

This strategy is about the importance of having a corporation. We're not talking about a Nevada Corporation yet. We're just talking about a regular corporation. I'm going to give you a list of reasons why I think corporations are good.

The number one reason why incorporation is so powerful, and the workhorse of this whole business enterprise is simply because the alternatives are not very good. Sole proprietorships, in particular, should be outlawed in my opinion.

Let me tell you what I do on a day-to-day basis. We help people set up their corporations and their limited partnerships. Every day we get great phone calls from people who are making money. However, most of the phone calls coming in aren't about the good stuff. They are about the bad stuff.

People call on the phone and say, "I went to your seminar eight years ago. It was wonderful. I loved it. I went out and made all this money, and now I'm getting sued," or, "Wade, I should have listened to you a long time ago. I went out and did it. I made a whole bunch of money, but now I'm getting killed on taxes, 40% of what I make is going to the government."

Had people taken time to do it right, to get financially fit for the opportunity, then they wouldn't have all these problems. The number one entity, the one that everybody needs is a corporation. Most people need two or three corporations to handle their different investments. They at least need one or two corporations for moving money from one state to another. They need corporations to have different tax brackets. They need to have corporations to protect their riches for their children to use for college, and to retire on later. There's so much that can be done with a corporation, and in a lot of ways corporations are light years ahead of a Living Trust for estate planning purposes. A Living Trust avoids probate, but a corporation provides other advantages.

Now for my list of reasons why I think corporations are so great:

1. Sole proprietorships are so bad. You go to these attorneys and they tell you to go ahead and be a sole proprietorship because you're not big enough to be a corporation. Well, now you have no tax planning vehicle at all. You have no lessening of your exposure to risk or liability. You have no ability to move money off from one year to another. You just minimized everything you could do by being in business as a sole proprietorship.

2. If you're ever going to do personal investments or run a business, the corporation helps you divide up your income and your assets into different legal entities, thereby lessening the risk of loss.

3. The risk or the exposure to liability by the officers, directors, and the shareholders, in most instances, is seriously reduced or eliminated by a corporation. You, as shareholder of your own family corporation, are not liable for the activities of the corporation. As an officer, if you do something illegal, then you may be held liable.

   If you run a corporation right, you set it up and you do it right: it takes title to businesses, it takes title to real estate or whatever, and if it's running and operating the right way and the books are accurate, then there's no way that somebody can go through the corporation and sue you. I know these attorneys talk about piercing the corporate veil, and I challenge them all the time to find me one case where it has happened. So far, no one has done it; that's just attorney talk. And, by the way, what's the alternative?

4. Corporations are eternal, they're perpetual in nature. Some of you right now are going to be setting up corporations that will be around 200 and 300 years from now. They'll support your kids, your grandkids, and your great grandkids in the businesses and enterprises that you're getting into. The corporation may outlive you.

5. From an estate planning point of view, corporations are phenomenal. They allow you to divide the stock in any way you choose to your kids and grandkids. You can have voting stock and nonvoting stock, and you as the parents keep the voting stock. You can have preferred stock and common stock.

You can divide small amounts to the parents in a corporation that's just getting started, and give huge amounts of stock to the kids. There's no tax consequence, because the stock is not really worth anything at the very beginning. When you put money into the corporation as a capital contribution or you can loan it to the corporation. As a loan you can get the money back in a year or two as a loan repayment and have no tax consequences. I could go on and on, but I think you get the point.

CHOOSE A NEVADA CORPORATION

Choose a Nevada Corporation. I just cannot stress the importance of this. It doesn't matter what state you are in, you should set up a Nevada Corporation. Why Nevada? Because in Nevada there's no corporate income tax, no stock transfer tax, no franchise tax, and no succession tax.

Don't get me wrong. If you do business in one state and you make a profit in that state, you will have to pay some business taxes on the profits there, but you will not have to pay taxes on money you make in other states. You will not have to pay taxes on money that you make on a national basis, like your investments.

For example, you could have a California company, but do that as a Nevada Corporation. Now, that Nevada Corporation could also have a brokerage account at a stock broker's office in Las Vegas so that none of the dividends or other income (option premium, et cetera) are being taxed in the State of California.

If you do business in California they tax you on any money you make in that state, any other state, in any other country in the world. California acts like a country in and of itself and not as a part of the United States of America. Several other states are moving in that direction. Taxes are a big reason for incorporation. Some say the only reason, but I think it's about 20% of the reason why you should be a Nevada Corporation.

In Nevada, the officers of a corporation cannot be sued for the activities of the corporation. These officers could be you and your wife, or you and a couple of friends that have set up a corporation. In Nevada, they simply legislated it out of existence–the officers cannot be sued for the activities of the corporation.

Also, Nevada is a total secrecy state–no one can find out who owns the stock in your company. Nevada is the only state that has not signed an information sharing agreement with the IRS.

In Nevada, anybody can own stock in the company, which means foreigners can own stock. To make a long story short, Nevada is the number one place.

Delaware used to be the number one state. By the way, in some of my books I do a side-by-side comparison of Nevada and Delaware. Delaware was the best for many, many years and it's now second best. Even if you were to compare the top two states in this country, Nevada and Delaware, Nevada would win hands down, but there really is no comparison. The list reads Nevada, Delaware, New Hampshire, Idaho, and then on down, with number 50 being California.

So no matter what state you are doing business in, you need to set up your legal structure in Nevada. If you domicile it there, you can do business in a myriad of states and you lessen a lot of exposure to risk.

I know the best company ever for setting up these Nevada Corporations. They set up a corporation with 25 million shares of stock. That's the authorized stock. We encourage you to issue a million shares. They set up the corporation in Nevada with redeemable stock so the company can buy back the stock.

Let's say, for example, one of your kids marries somebody that you don't like. You can buy back the stock at par value. So, if you've issued 200,000 shares of stock to that child, you can buy that stock back at $200 because the par value is at .001. We set it up with preferred stock and common stock, which nobody else does.

Make sure that your corporation does for you what you really want it to do. For a free seminar cassette, call 1-800-706-4741.

LIVING TRUSTS

We're going move away from the corporations. From time to time we'll come back to corporations and how they work in regard to these other legal entities and how they are integrated together.

Has anybody noticed that Living Trust seminars are kind of a phenomenon of the last few years? You didn't see them seven, eight, nine, or ten years ago. I've been teaching Living Trust seminars for over a decade. What I see is a lot of these ambulance chasing attorneys now jumping on the bandwagon. Most of these people do not see the whole picture. They understand the basics of a Living Trust, but they don't understand how limited these trusts are and yet how wonderful they can be.

The reason that Living Trusts have really gotten popular is because of the problems of probate. Even though some states have streamlined the probate process, it is still a horrible, ugly process.

When someone dies, if they own things, in order to transfer those things from one person to another it has to go before a court. Now, I believe that a will is the most dangerous document in this country, because it lulls people into a state of complacency. People think that because they have a will everything is going to be taken care of. Nothing could be further from the truth.

All wills, 100% of them, have to go through the probate process. So having a will is just slightly better than not having a will. By the way, why do you think attorneys will write up a will for you for $50 and keep it in their safe deposit box for the next 40 years waiting for you to die? Because they want to get their claws into everything you have owned. I mean, your estate is their retirement vehicle—and believe me, you want to keep your estate and your affairs out of the hands of attorneys upon your death.

The only way to avoid probate is to not die. If you do die, there's another really, really good way that almost assures that you'll avoid the probate process. Here is it: die as a pauper. If you have nothing to transfer there will be no probate. Think this one through: you die as a pauper; you don't have anything. You could work for and control $10 million or $100 million in assets, but none of that is in your own personal name. How do you set it up so you can do that? Well, you put everything that you own (remember that 5% of the stock in one of those corporation and 2% in another corporation that you and your wife own) into a Living Trust. The trust now owns your stock.

Upon your death the trustee, whoever you choose to handle your affairs when you're not here, steps in and takes control of the company. You don't have anything in your estate, and there's no cause for probate. Everything has been transferred before you die.

While you're alive, you're going to set this trust up as a Living Trust, an inter vivos trust. You may want to make changes to it from time to time, so you'll set it up as a revocable trust. That is really two different trusts, which today is actually a hybrid trust of those two. Sometimes, it's referred to as a family trust, which is pretty much the same thing.

A Living Trust has two functions upon your death. One function is to keep everything together. Those things that you want to keep together those things that will support your family and pay for your kids to go to college. The other thing that the trust does is to give things away, just like a will. "I give to my son the '57 Chevy, I give to my daughter the jewelry"—the trust provides a vehicle for giving things away.

It gives certain things away and it keeps certain things together for your family. Eventually, the Living Trust is going to end; it will disburse everything when your children get older, but a Living Trust is remarkable because it avoids probate.

Now remember the three reasons for estate planning: the first is to avoid probate, the second is to avoid or reduce estate taxes, and the third is to provide for the continuity of your assets. That's what this does. Living Trusts are great. Now let me just give you a few other items that you need to make sure of. (This is where a lot of these attorneys go wrong.)

1. A Living Trust needs to be fully funded. You need to have everything put into the Living Trust, everything you own. From now on *you* cease to exist. You don't have anything in your own name. When you go to the movies you're going with Living Trust money. When you buy groceries you're buying groceries with Living Trust money. Everything you do, you do as a Living Trust. The Living Trust is really you while you're alive. Now, you, as the husband and wife, are the co-trustees of this trust and you handle your everyday affairs; just remember, it needs to be fully funded.

2. In case you forgot to put something in the Living Trust before you died, there is a document called a Joint Pour-Over Will, or a Pour-Over Will, which pours over, into the Living Trust upon your death, anything you forgot to put in the Living Trust. Is this the answer? You need this Joint Pour-Over Will, but you should never have to use it, because your Living Trust truly needs to be fully funded.

3. This is where another big gap exists in the Living Trusts prepared by most attorneys. If you use us to set up your Living Trust, we will set it up with what is called a cata-strophic illness clause in case, for example, you were to get seriously ill, and have $300,000 or $400,000 in doctor bills.

   If you apply for Medicaid and your financial statements show you're worth quite a bit of money they'll say, "Just sell off your assets to pay the bills." Now watch what happens: if you or your wife were to get sick, you and your wife could decide to execute this catastrophic clause. At that point in time the husband's or the wife's half of the trust becomes irrevocable; it becomes a grantor trust. Everything in that trust is now held by the trust, and it has nothing to do with the ownership of the husband or the wife at that point in time.

Let's say it's the husband that is sick. Now, his half of the Living Trust is irrevocable, and the wife's half is still a revocable Living Trust. When he goes in to apply for Medicaid and they ask him how much his house is worth, he can reply, "Zero." Again, when they ask him how much his investments are worth—zero. You see, he doesn't have anything. Everything is out of his name and now qualifies for full Medicaid. Living Trusts are really great because they can solve problems in the future and protect assets.

4. This last one is really, really important. If you own a house in a joint tenancy as a husband and wife, which, by the way, is not quite as good as owning as tenants in common, and which is nowhere near as good as owning your house as a Living Trust. You lose some tax advantages. If you live in a community property state, a lot of the things that I'm going to show you right now are available to you. But let's talk about joint tenancy.

You own a house in joint tenancy; you bought it many, many years ago for $100,000. The house today is worth $500,000. Upon the death of the husband, the wife goes to sell the house because she doesn't want to live there anymore. She sells it for $500,000, and the IRS steps in and says they need to determine what taxes are due on the deal. They will want to know how she owned the house. It was owned in joint tenancy.

If not in a community property state and owned in joint tenancy, they just divide the house in half. What is her basis? Her basis in the property is $50,000, or half of the $100,000 original purchase price. Then they allow her to receive the husband's basis at the time of his death. The house is worth $500,000 when he died. His basis then would have been $250,000. She sells the house for $500,000, her basis is $50,000, her husband's basis is $250,000, add those two together and you have a $300,000 basis in the property. If in a community property state, her basis becomes the fair market value of the house at the time of her husband's death.

There is no longer a one time exemption. Instead, there is a $500,000 gain exclusion for married couples who own real property and live in the property for two of the last five years, regardless of age.

Let's do it a second way—don't own the house in joint tenancy. (By the way, I dislike joint tenancy immensely.) You own the house between the husband and wife in a Living Trust. Upon the death of the husband, the wife sells the house for $500,000 as co-trustee of the Living Trust.

In steps the IRS: they need to determine what the capital gains are. Again, they want to know how the house was owned. It was assigned to a Living Trust; the wife receives the house. How much was it worth when her husband died? It was worth $500,000. All right, she gets to receive it at the full stepped up basis, not half. The wife sells it for $500,000. The full stepped up, or new basis is $500,000, and she has zero capital gains and no taxes to pay.

These Living Trusts are really sharp. They really function well. Most of the attorneys that teach Living Trust seminars have no idea of the consequences or the tax liabilities and the tax savings afforded by a Living Trust. They're really quite remarkable. You need to have one. By the way, if the wife stays living in the house, and sells it later for $600,000, she has now established a new basis of $500,000 at the time of her husband's death. In that scenario she'd have a $100,000 capital gain.

A GREAT RETIREMENT

This section is about getting ready for a great retirement and setting up a retirement entity for flexibility and diversified investing. You've heard of tax free investments, like municipal bonds and some other investments that produce cash flow, tax write offs, and growth, but how would you like to have an entity set up that takes everything that you would ever get involved in—everything—and turn it all into a tax free investment?

You have a few choices. One choice is to set up an IRA. I believe that everybody should have an IRA, even if you cannot deduct the standard $2,000. You should also set up IRAs for your children, and if you have a company pay your children each $2,000 to work for your company, then put that whole $2,000 into an IRA. Think about what you just did—you expensed $2,000 out of your company, so there is less tax, but now the $2,000 is going into an IRA for one of your children and will grow tax free.

The second choice is a SEP-IRA—Simplified Employee Pension IRA. If you're self-employed or a sole proprietorship, you can sock aside up to $30,000 into a SEP-IRA. If you're self-employed you can set up a more elaborate Keogh plan. I like a Keogh plans for sole proprietorships, and a corporate Pension Plan for corporations.

The plan that gives you the maximum strength, maximum protection, and maximum power is a corporate pension. There are many, many reasons for having one. I love corporations because they can take advantage of having this great Pension Plan. You can put away more money, repeatedly.

In a corporation you can set aside huge amounts of money. Based on the compensation that you're paying yourself, your wife, or any of your employees, you can put aside up to $30,000 per year per person. That's $30,000 for the husband and $30,000 for the wife. This amount becomes a tax write off, right now; it's a donation.

You also get to be the trustee of this plan. What does that mean? It means that you've got the checkbook. It's in your glove box, it's in your purse, and you're out working your investments.

So you set up this tax free entity, you get the tax deductions, and now you've got the checkbook. If you have a Pension Plan set up at Charles Schwab or Dean Witter or Merrill Lynch, as I've said before you're limited on what you can do. You can do what they allow you to do, and this may vary from firm to firm, if you use the cash flow formulas mentioned in this book. However, they mey only allow you to do stocks, mutual funds, Rolling Stocks, and writing covered calls. You may still be able to make a lot of money with these strategies, especially if you do the Rolling Stocks plan, but why not have the checkbook?

What I'm talking about is called a self trusteed plan, where nobody else touches your money. You keep control of your money and put your financial destiny into your own hands. Think about this: a lot of people ask me what a trust is, as if a trust were a thing. A trust is not a thing.

A trust is a relationship between three people. There is a trustor, that's the person who sets it up and usually funds it; there's the trustee, that's the person that takes care of the money; and there's the beneficiary. In most trust situations these three people are different. For example, if you want to give money to your kids, you set up a trust, you put the money into a bank, the bank takes care of the money as the trustee, and your kids get it later on. But think about this one.

In the Pension Plan I'm using here, who's the trustor? You are. You're the corporation that sets up the Pension Plan. Who's the trustee? You are, you've got the checkbook. And who's the beneficiary? You are. You're the trustor, the trustee and the beneficiary of the same money. It doesn't get more exciting than this, because you control all the money going in, how much you're going to put in, you control the money once it's in, and you can control the money coming out. That's pretty exciting!

The entity that you should be using to get wealthy is a retirement entity. Most people have never thought this way. They're always trying to build up their company and get their company rich, or to build up their own personal net worth and get themselves rich. But why not sock aside money into a pension account and have the pension account get rich.

A lot of the strategies that I've written about in the stock market are incredible strategies, but why not do the ones you can in a Pension Plan? Why not buy and sell, do the Range Riders, do the Rolling Stocks, invest for dividends, and increase the return on your money because it is growing tax free.

USE A VARIETY OF ENTITIES

Use a variety of these different entities. For example, you can have a Keogh plan, but if you have a Keogh plan then you do not qualify for a SEP-IRA. You can have an IRA and you can put aside the $2,000 into an IRA. I've helped people, for example, set up a corporate Pension Plan for one of their businesses, but they had another business that was a partnership with their children. They set up a plan there, and they're putting aside money for their children in the partnership plan. Use these different types of retirement accounts to have your investments—that's diversity.

The next thing is that you need to diversify your investments. You need to get involved in a variety of different things. Now, please understand that I really believe that the Pension Plan should have a mission, it should have a theme, it should have a central area that it focuses on.

For example, if you're going to get good at Rolling Stocks, then have your Pension Plan buy and sell those three or four stocks that you're really good at. If you're going to do mutual funds, get really good at mutual funds. Study them. A Pension Plan should have a theme, but while it has a lot of its money tied up in one central type of investment, it can also get involved in things like limited partnership units and some real estate investments or other kinds of debt. It can buy bonds. By the way, a perfect type of investment would be the zero coupon bond. Remember one of the problems with zeros is phantom income? Well, you don't have to worry about phantom income in the Pension Plan, because it pays no taxes. Buy a zero coupon bond that will mature when you're 65, and a big one to mature when you're 70. You want to have a good time and travel the world when you're 70, so buy a bunch of bonds today that will mature when you're 70, and then you pull them out of the Pension Plan at that point in time.

I could just spend whole days talking about the flexibility, the freedom and the power it brings you when you understand investing this way—investing in an entity that pays no taxes. Every other way you have to pay taxes to the IRS. If you get rich under a corporation, it has to pay taxes. The Pension Plan just sits there and waves at the IRS on April 15th. So, the pension entity is the entity that you should use.

LIMITED PARTNERSHIPS

Let me show you how to gift away assets. If you have stock in a corporation, you can just start gifting away the stock. If you have units or stock in a trust, you can start gifting that away also. But the entity that I'd like to share with you right now is a limited partnership. We're going to call it a Family Limited Partnership, because a lot of times only family members are involved.

The word limited means limited liability–if ten investors put in $10,000 to form a partnership to buy an apartment complex, they have $100,000. Let's say I'm the general partner and I take the investors' $100,000 and invest it. Now, let's say I forget to get insurance on it, the place burns down and we lose everything. What could you lose? You're limited in your liability; you can lose your $10,000. What about me? I can lose everything, I'm the general partner. I have general liability. They could put liens on my house, I could lose my business, I could lose everything.

When I see a man setting up a limited partnership my hat goes off to him. By the way, I'm the least chauvinistic guy you'll ever meet. Why did I say "man" there? I've been reviewing limited partnerships for over 17 years now. I've reviewed over 300 limited partnerships, and to this day not one time have I seen a woman be the general partner. Not one time. Now why is that? Well, I think they're too smart. I think that women realize that if they're going to put their necks on the line and risk losing everything, they're not going to get involved.

I just bad mouthed being the general partner, but you still need to be the general partner. Male or female, you need to be the general partner. Simply put, you control the checkbook. You need to have the checkbook for this partnership, so you can control the type of the investments and the direction of the company.

Limited partnerships can run businesses, they can have investments. They have their own federal ID number, they can have a brokerage account; in short they become a separate legal entity. I like limited partnerships; I like them almost as much as corporations. A limited partnership can't have an off year-end like a corporation can have, but they're still limited in liability, just like a corporation is. The tax consequences of limited partnerships are really exciting–a limited partnership pays no taxes in and of itself.

Say that you own 5% of a partnership, your wife owns 5%, one of your kids owns 17%, another one owns 33%, and you have even given 20% to your mother and your father who are in their 60s or 70s. You gift out all these units. At the end of the year, if this partnership has made $100,000 in profits, the money is taxed down to the limited partners by their respective share of ownership. There are no taxes at the partnership level. By the way, when we set up a limited partnership for people, we set it up with 100,000 units, and are then divvied up among the different people by percentages.

Don't get me wrong, you don't have to actually give your money to the kids; your kids never see a dime of this money. It's just allocated to them in their tax brackets, and the money just goes into your own household checking account. You're buying groceries with it; you're going to the movies with it. The point is that the partnership is not taxed. It fills out an information return, a Form 1065, but the money is taxed down to the individual partners.

Let's say that you currently are worth a lot of money. You could set up a limited partnership for running a business; it has no assets of its own. It's a cash flow entity. It has a business, or it manages another business. It just receives money and distributes money. That's one way of getting money into different tax brackets. But, let's say that you do have existing assets: $600,000, $1 million, maybe even $2 million.

First of all, I really believe that if you're worth $2 to $3 million you should have multiple corporations. I don't think any one entity should own over 20% of all of your investments. You should have at least five different legal entities.

For example, if you are worth $1 million, you should have three corporations and two limited partnerships that have about $200,000 equity in each of them. You could also set up a fourth corporation. If you have a lot of equity in another corporation or a lot of equity in your personal residence, with a corporation or a limited partnership you could put a deed of trust or a mortgage against your own personal residence. You could encumber all of the equity in your house, so if anybody ever sues you, they can never get at any of the equity. You do that as a trade.

You trade stock in a corporation and give it to your kids or your grandkids. Then you put a lien against the property in the name of the corporation and record the deed so that you can never ever lose the equity in your property.

Now, let's get back to the partnership and I'll show you what being invincible means from a couple of different angles. For example, you take your $2 million and put it into several partnerships. You deed, you assign, you transfer $2 million into the partnerships. Now the units are divided. If you do it this way and you own everything, all the investments in the partnership, in this example the 100,000 units probably would have gone 50,000 to mom and 50,000 to dad when the partnership was first set up. Now, think this one through, these are units. You have a ledger in the back of your partnership book and you have 100,000 units, 50,000 to mom, 50,000 to dad. Can mom now give some of her units away? Figure out how much her units are worth and she can give them all away, but with no tax consequences. She could give away $10,000 worth these units per year. She takes $10,000 and deeds them, or assigns them to her children. Every year she gives away $10,000. You see what we've just done? We've now set up an entity that allows you to take control of your investments outside of your personal name, have the units owned by the mom and the dad, and then gift them away to the kids. Mom and dad are still the general partners. They are still in control

They should keep 1% of the partnership units no matter what, but they could gift away 99% of all the units to their children, to their grandchildren, to their own mom and dad. They could give away everything, and still control the whole entity. They draw out salaries, they decide how much is going into Pension Plans, they have full control.

Now, let's see if we've solved the problem of gifting. The gifting problem was that you don't have neat packages in $10,000 groups of assets. That problem is gone, because now you have nice, neat little groups of assets that you can give away.

When all the gifting is completed you still want to live that big happy life, you still control all the money in the partnership. See, the partnership now owns the investments, owns the rental properties, owns your businesses, et cetera. By the way, just to avoid personal liability, when you set up your Limited Partnership make sure that your Nevada Corporation is the general partner. So your corporation, not you, is the general partner. This gives you another way of moving money out of state to a Nevada brokerage or bank account. This lessens your taxes, and you've avoided all personal liability.

Charitable Remainder Trusts

I very seldom get excited about a legal entity like I am about the Charitable Remainder Trust. This is a phenomenal entity with a little twist to it that makes it really exciting. There are four kinds of trusts. Most of them don't work for what I'm going to show you.

What I'm talking about is a Charitable Remainder Unitrust (or CRUT). Let's say you're making $50,000 a year, you've got some investments, some rental properties, and a brokerage account. You can set up a charitable remainder unitrust–technically, it's called a split interest trust.

The split interest in this trust is going to be this: you will be the income beneficiary and you'll choose a charity to get the investments that you place into the trust when you die. That will be the charity beneficiary. This charity beneficiary could be your church– I recommend that, because you have 30% and 50% charities. The government has an approved list of 50% charities, and churches fall into the 50% category. You donate to this charity some appreciated stock or real estate. You're the trustee of this trust, you control all the investments held in trust, which could have been a rental property or anything else. You sell that property for cash.

The point is that you now get a $100,000 donation. You get to take a portion of this donation against current income. Think about what I just said: you've been able to take something and give it to a charity that you really like, that you want to have the money later on, but you get a deduction right now, and an incredible savings off your income tax.

Now, if you take a $25,000 deduction this year, and you donated a $100,000 asset, you still have $75,000. So you take some of the deduction next year, and so on until that $100,000 is used up. Later on you could even donate something else. You can continue making donations to this trust which will eventually go to the charity.

Now, each year, because you're the income beneficiary, you have to pull out 5%, even up to 15%, but you have to take out at least 5% of the assets. So, if you have $100,000 in there, you need to pull out $5,000. But hold it, we're going to show you a real neat angle to this.

If you use us to set up your CRT–Charitable Remainder Trust– we'll set it up with what is called "make-up provision." What this means is that if you cannot pull out the money, if there's no income in the trust now, you'll be able to take that income when those assets eventually make money. So you have this makeup provision in the trust to control when you actually will take out income–now or later.

You've also now lessened your estate. If you put all these donations into the charity, based on what they could have been worth in your own estate, your family will not have to pay estate taxes. You've donated them to the Charitable Remainder Trust, and it's outside of your estate now because this is a grantor trust, or irrevocable trust. You can't get the assets back out.

First of all, this should not have been your only entity. You should still have a Living Trust and other entities to take care of your family. This one is for the excess things that you want to go to a charity upon your death. Look what you have done: You take deductions now; lessen your estate upon your death, make sure your kids are taken care of, profit by incredible cash flow for yourself either now and/or in the future; and your favorite charity gets this final tithing on your life. This CRT is a phenomenal way to go.

INTEGRATING YOUR ENTITIES

This strategy is about the integration of all of these entities. There are three basic entities, and two others which I really think are important. The three basic entities are the Corporation, the Living Trust, and the Pension Plan. Those are the three basic entities that everybody needs. The other entities that you can pick and choose from are the Limited Partnership and the Charitable Remainder Trust. Now this explanation has been brief. To better understand these entities and how they work together please order our Financial Fortress Home Study Course, come to a B.E.S.T. (Business Entity Skills Training), or our extensive Wealth Institute.

For example, the corporation can be the general partner of the partnership. A partnership can own stock in a corporation. The stock that you also own in a corporation could and should be owned by your Living Trust, in order to make sure that none of the stock is in your own name.

You could take one corporation and put liens against your other corporation, or put liens against your personal residence to avoid any threat of lawsuits, and even if you do get sued you won't lose any of your equity. You can integrate these entities in so many ways that there's no way that I can do justice to all of them in this book.

I also have a good video tape of this, that is part of a bonus included with the Financial Fortress set of books and tapes. It's called the Entity Integration Video. It's about an hour and a half of me actually designing and diagramming these different entities, as you watch. I encourage you to sit down and take time to structure yourself, and learn how these entities interact with each other.

TAKING CARE OF YOU

Take care of "You"–nobody is going to do this for you. You imagine tonight your CPA getting home, snuggling down into bed, pulling his covers up around his neck, and tell me how much he's worried about your financial situation. You need to set these things up and do them yourself. You need to get going. You need to not only understand these different entities but control setting them up.

If my company can be of help in doing these things; if we can help you get these things structured so that you are financially fit and so you can sleep when the wind blows, then great. We'd love to be of service.

APPENDIX 3

AVAILABLE RESOURCES

The following books, videos, and audiocassettes have been reviewed by the Wade Cook Seminars, Inc., Lighthouse Publishing Group, Inc. or Gold Press Leaf staff and are suggested as reading and resource material for continuing education to help with your financial planning, and real estate and stock market investments. Because new ideas and techniques come along and laws change, we're always updating our catalog.

To order a copy of our current catalog, please write or call us at:

Wade Cook Seminars, Inc.
14675 Interurban Avenue South
Seattle, Washington 98168-4664
1-800-872-7411

Or, visit us on our web sites at:
www.wadecook.com
www.lighthousebooks.com

Also, we would love to hear your comments on our products and services, as well as your testimonials on how these products have benefited you. We look forward to hearing from you!

AUDIOCASSETTES

13 FANTASTIC INCOME FORMULAS—A FREE CASSETTE
Presented by Wade B. Cook
Learn 13 cash flow formulas, some of which are taught in the Wall Street Workshop™. Learn to double some of your money in 2¹/₂ to 4 months.

ZERO TO ZILLIONS
Presented by Wade B. Cook
A four-album, 16-cassette, powerful audio workshop on Wall Street—understanding it, playing it successfully, and retiring rich. Learn 11 powerful investment strategies as you drive. Learn to avoid pitfalls and losses. Learn to catch "day-trippers" and how to "bottom fish." Learn to write covered calls and to possibly double your money in one week on options on stock split companies. Wade "Meter Drop" Cook can teach you how he makes 300% per year in his accounts. You then will have the information to try to follow suit. Each album comes with a workbook, and the entire workshop includes a free bonus video called "Dynamic Dollars," 90 minutes of instruction on how all the strategies can be integrated, and giving actual examples of what kinds of returns are possible so you can get in there and play the market successfully. A must for every savvy, would-be investor.

POWER OF NEVADA CORPORATIONS—A FREE CASSETTE
Presented by Wade B. Cook
Nevada Corporations have secrecy, privacy, minimal taxes, no reciprocity with the IRS, and protection for shareholders, officers, and directors. This is a powerful seminar.

INCOME STREAMS—A FREE CASSETTE
Presented by Wade B. Cook
Learn to buy and sell real estate the Wade Cook way. This informative cassette will instruct you in building and operating your own real estate money machine.

MONEY MYSTERIES OF THE MILLIONAIRES—A FREE CASSETTE
Presented by Wade B. Cook

How to make money and keep it. This fantastic seminar shows you how to use Nevada Corporations, Living Trusts, Pension Plans, Charitable Remainder Trusts, and Family Limited Partnerships to protect your assets.

24 KARAT
Presented by Wade B. Cook

Learn how to protect your family's finances through anything—including Y2K! 24 Karat seminar on cassette teaches people how currency fluctuates and the safest currency to have. This seminar is packed with must-know information about your future.

HIGH-IMPACT TRADING
Presented by Steve Wirrick

This highly sought-after home study course will introduce you to a few of the insider secrets every trader should know. High-Impact Trading will help you better identify and capture explosive profits, minimize losses, and avoid the stress and worry normally associated with trading. Whether you're a seasoned pro or brand new to option investing, you'll find this course to be an invaluable educational tool.

HIGH OCTANE OPTIONS
Presented by Steve Wirrick

During the taping of this live seminar, Steve shared his favorite tips and techniques for making money in the options market. Even if you have never traded or made money with stocks or options before, you can soon learn how to make quick profits with the help of "High Octane Options."

UNLIMITED WEALTH AUDIO SET
By Wade B. Cook

Unlimited Wealth is the "University of Money-Making Ideas" home study course that helps you improve your money's personality. The heart and soul of this seminar is to make more money, pay fewer taxes, and keep more for your retirement and family. This cassette series contains the great ideas from *Wealth 101* on tape, so you can listen to them whenever you want.

RETIREMENT PROSPERITY
By Wade B. Cook

Take that IRA money now sitting idle and invest it in ways that generate you bigger, better, and quicker returns. This four audiotape set walks you through a system of using a self directed IRA to create phenomenal profits, virtually tax free! This is one of the most complete systems for IRA investing ever created.

THE FINANCIAL FORTRESS HOME STUDY COURSE
By Wade B. Cook

This eight-part series is the last word in entity structuring. It goes far beyond mere financial planning or estate planning. It helps you structure your business and your affairs so that you can avoid the majority of taxes, retire rich, escape lawsuits, bequeath your assets to your heirs without government interference, and, in short, bomb-proof your entire estate. There are six audio cassette seminars on tape, an entity structuring video, and a full kit of documents.

PAPER TIGERS AND PAPER CHASE
Presented by Wade B. Cook

Wade gives you a personal introduction to the art of buying and selling real estate. In this set of six cassettes, Wade shares his inside secrets to establishing a cash flow business with real estate investments. You will learn how to find discounted second mortgages, second mortgage notes, and make them better, as well as how you can get 40%-plus yields on your money. Learn the art of structuring your business to attract investors and bring in the income you desire through the use of family corporations, pension plans, and other entities.

When you buy Paper Tigers, you'll also receive Paper Chase for free. Paper Chase holds the most important tools you need to make deals happen. Wade created these powerful tapes as a handout tool you can lend to potential investors or home owners to help educate them about how this amazing cash flow system works for them. It explains how you'll negotiate a lower interest rate if they make a larger payment. You will use this incredible tool over and over again.

THE REAL ESTATE CASH FLOW SYSTEM
Presented by Wade B. Cook

This six-volume audiocassette set, originally sold separately, contains everything you'll ever need to begin investing in real estate immediately, do so successfully, handle all of the business aspects and retire sooner than you ever thought possible. Just look at all the tremendous information that can be yours.

BOOKS

WALL STREET MONEY MACHINE
By Wade B. Cook

Appearing on the New York Times Business Best-Sellers List for over one year, *Wall Street Money Machine* contains the best strategies for wealth enhancement and cash flow creation you'll find anywhere. Throughout this book, Wade Cook describes many of his favorite strategies for generating cash flow through the stock market: Rolling Stocks, Proxy Investing, Covered Calls, and many more. It's a great introduction for creating wealth using the Wade Cook formulas.

STOCK MARKET MIRACLES
By Wade B. Cook

The anxiously-awaited partner to *Wall Street Money Machine*, this book is proven to be just as invaluable. *Stock Market Miracles* improves on some of the strategies from *Wall Street Money Machine*, as well as introduces new and valuable twists on our old favorites. This is a must read for anyone interested in making money in the stock market.

BEAR MARKET BALONEY
By Wade B. Cook

A more timely book wouldn't be possible. Wade's predictions came true while the book was at press! Don't miss this insightful look into what makes bull and bear markets and how to make exponential returns in any market.

ON TRACK INVESTING
By David R. Hebert

On Track Investing is the instruction book for novice stock market investors or anyone wanting to practice investment strategies without risking actual cash. Combined with your personal game plan, the Simutrade™ System helps you originate good trades, perfect your timing, and check your open trades against your personal criteria. There are Simutrade™ Worksheets and step by step guides for ten strategies. *On Track Investing* helps you develop a step by step map of what exactly you're going to do and how you're going to accomplish it.

ROLLING STOCKS
By Gregory Witt

Rolling Stocks shows you the simplest and most powerful strategy for profiting from the ups and down of the stock market. You'll learn how to find rolling stocks, get in smoothly at the right price, and time your exit. You will recognize the patterns of rolling stocks and how to make the most money from these strategies. Apply rolling stock principles to improve your trading options and fortify your portfolio.

SLEEPING LIKE A BABY
By John C. Hudelson

Perhaps the most predominant reason people don't invest in the stock market is fear. *Sleeping Like A Baby* removes the fear from investing and gives you the confidence and knowledge to invest wisely, safely, and profitably.

You'll learn how to build a high quality portfolio and plan for your future and let your investments follow. Begin to invest as early as possible, and use proper asset allocation and diversification to reduce risk.

MAKING A LIVING IN THE STOCK MARKET
By Bob Eldridge

In simplistic, easy to understand terms and presentation, Bob Eldridge will show you how you can change your job and your life by *Making A Living In The Stock Market*. This powerful book is full of real life examples of profitable trades. Pages full of charts, diagrams, and tables help the reader understand exactly how these strategies are implemented.

If you live for your job, have little or no money at the end of each paycheck, and have forgotten your dreams in days gone past, this book is for you. In *Making A Living In The Stock Market*, you can learn how to make money with cash generating strategies including: channeling stock prices, covered calls, selling naked puts, selling naked calls, call (debit) spread, put (credit) spread, and stock splits.

101 WAYS TO BUY REAL ESTATE WITHOUT CASH
By Wade B. Cook

Wade Cook has personally achieved success after success in real estate. *101 Ways To Buy Real Estate Without Cash* fills the gap left by other authors who have given all the ingredients but not the whole recipe for real estate investing. This is the book for the investor who wants innovative and practical methods for buying real estate with little or no money down.

COOK'S BOOK ON CREATIVE REAL ESTATE
By Wade B. Cook

Make your real estate buying experiences profitable and fun. *Cook's Book On Creative Real Estate* will show you how! You will learn suggestions for finding the right properties, buying them quickly, and profiting even quicker.

HOW TO PICK UP FORECLOSURES
By Wade B. Cook

Do you want to become an expert money maker in real estate? This book will show you how to buy real estate at 60¢ on the dollar or less. You'll learn to find the house before the auction and purchase it with no bank financing–the easy way to millions in real estate. The market for foreclosures is a tremendous place to learn and prosper. *How To Pick Up Foreclosures* takes Wade's methods from *Real Estate Money Machine* and supercharges them by applying the fantastic principles to already-discounted properties.

OWNER FINANCING
By Wade B. Cook

This is a short but invaluable booklet you can give to sellers who hesitate to sell you their property using the owner financing method. Let this pamphlet convince both you and them. The special report, "Why Sellers Should Take Monthly Payments," is included for free!

REAL ESTATE FOR REAL PEOPLE
By Wade B. Cook

A priceless, comprehensive overview of real estate investing, this book teaches you how to buy the right property for the right price, at the right time. Wade Cook explains all of the strategies you'll need and gives you 20 reasons why you should start investing in real estate today. Learn how to retire rich with real estate, and have fun doing it.

REAL ESTATE MONEY MACHINE
By Wade B. Cook

Wade's first bestselling book reveals the secrets of Wade Cook's own system—the system he earned his first million from. This book teaches you how to make money regardless of the state of the economy. Wade's innovative concepts for investing in real estate not only avoids high interest rates, but avoids banks altogether.

BLUEPRINTS FOR SUCCESS, VOLUME 1
Contributors: Wade Cook, Debbie Losse, Joel Black, Dan Wagner, Tim Semingson, Rich Simmons, Greg Witt, JJ Childers, Keven Hart, Dave Wagner and Steve Wirrick

Blueprints for Success, Volume 1 is a compilation of chapters on building your wealth through your business and making your business function successfully. The chapters cover education and information gathering, choosing the best business for you from all the different types of business, and a variety of other skills necessary for becoming successful. Your business can't afford to miss these powerful insights!

BRILLIANT DEDUCTIONS
By Wade B. Cook

Do you want to make the most of the money you earn? Do you want to have solid tax havens and ways to reduce the taxes you pay? This book is for you! Learn how to get rich in spite of the tax laws. See new tax credits, year-end maneuvers, and methods for transferring and controlling your entities. Learn to structure yourself and your family for tax savings and liability protection.

MILLION HEIRS
By John V. Childers Jr.

In his reader-friendly style, attorney John V. Childers Jr. explains how you can prepare your loved ones for when you pass away. He explains many details you need to take care of right away, before a death occurs, as well as strategies for your heirs to utilize. Don't leave your loved ones unprepared–get *Million Heirs*.

THE SECRET MILLIONAIRE GUIDE TO NEVADA CORPORATIONS
By John V. Childers Jr.

What does it mean to be a secret millionaire? In *The Secret Millionaire Guide To Nevada Corporations*, attorney John V. Childers Jr. outlines exactly how you can use some of the secret, extraordinary business tactics used by many of today's super-wealthy to protect your assets from the ravages of lawsuits and other destroyers using Nevada Corporations. You'll understand why the state of Nevada has become the preferred jurisdiction for those desiring to establish corporations and how to utilize Nevada Corporations for your financial benefit.

WEALTH 101
By Wade B. Cook

This incredible book brings you 101 strategies for wealth creation and protection that you can't afford to miss. Front to back, it is packed full of tips and tricks to supercharge your financial health. If you need to generate more cash flow, this book shows you how through several various avenues. If you are already wealthy, this is the book that will show you strategy upon strategy for decreasing your tax liability and increasing your peace of mind through liability protection.

A+
By Wade B. Cook

A+ is a collection of wisdom, thoughts, and principles of success which can help you make millions, even billions of dollars and live an A+ life. As you will see, Wade Cook consistently tries to live his life "in the second mile," to do more than asked, to be above normal.

If you want to live a successful life, you need great role models to follow. For years, Wade Cook's life has been a quest to find successful characteristics of his role models and implement them in his own life. In *A+*, Wade will encourage you to find and incorporate the most succesful principles and characteristics of success in your life, too. Don't spend another day living less than an A+ life!

BUSINESS BUY THE BIBLE
By Wade B. Cook

Inspired by the Creator, the Bible truly is the authority for running the business of life. Throughout *Business Buy The Bible*, you are provided with practical advice that helps you apply God's word to your life. You'll learn how you can apply God's words to saving, spending and investing, and how you can control debt instead of being controlled by it. You'll also learn how to use God's principles in your daily business activities and prosper.

DON'T SET GOALS
By Wade B. Cook

Don't Set Goals will teach you to be a goal-getter, not just a goal-setter. You'll learn that achieving goals is the result of prioritizing and acting. *Don't Set Goals* shows you how taking action and "paying the price" is more important than simply making the decision to do something. Don't just set goals. Go out and get your goals, go where you want to go!

WADE COOK'S POWER QUOTES, VOLUME 1
By Wade B. Cook

Wade Cook's Power Quotes, Volume 1 is chock full of exciting quotes that have motivated and inspired Mr. Cook. Wade Cook continually asks his students, "To whom are you listening?" He knows that if you get your advice and inspiration from successful people, you'll become successful yourself. He compiled *Wade Cook's Power Quotes, Volume 1* to provide you with a millionaire-on-call when you need advice.

LIVING IN COLOR
By Renae Knapp

Renae Knapp is the leading authority on the Blue Base/Yellow Base Color System and is recognized worldwide for her research and contribution to the study of color. Industries, universities, and men and women around the globe use Renae's tried and true–scientifically proven–system to achieve measurable results.

In *Living In Color*, Renae Knapp teaches you easy to understand methods which empower you to get more from your life by harnessing the power of color. In an engaging, straightforward way, Renae Knapp teaches the scientific Blue Base/Yellow Base Color System and how to achieve harmony and peace using color. You will develop a mastery of color harmony and an awareness of the amazing role color plays in every area of your life.

Y2K Gold Rush
By Wade B. Cook

As we approach the end of the millennium, newspapers and television newscasters drone on about Y2K. Computers will read the year 2000 as 1900! The issue is a definite problem, but in *Y2K Gold Rush*, Wade Cook discounts the need for this hysteria. First, businesses and individuals alike have been preparing for this problem. Secondly, and more importantly, people are now buying gold to protect themselves against all types of potential problems.

This book is about how to invest in gold. By reading *Y2K Gold Rush*, you will understand the historical importance of gold. You will learn about the ownership of gold coins and gold stocks, and the benefits of both. You will see that adding gold to your investment portfolio will diversify your assets, safeguard you and your family against catastrophe, and add excitement and profits.

VIDEOS

Dynamic Dollars Video
By Wade B. Cook

Wade Cook's 90 minute introduction to the basics of his Wall Street formulas and strategies. In this presentation designed especially for video, Wade explains the meter drop philosophy, Rolling Stocks, basics of Proxy Investing, and writing Covered Calls. Perfect for anyone looking for a little basic information.

The Wall Street Workshop™ Video Series
By Wade B. Cook

If you can't make it to the Wall Street Workshop™ soon, get a head start with these videos. Ten albums containing 11 hours of intense instruction on Rolling Stocks, options on stock split companies, writing Covered Calls, and ten other tested and proven strategies designed to help you increase the value of your investments. By learning, reviewing, and implementing the strategies taught here, you will gain the knowledge and the confidence to take control of your investments and get your money to work hard for you.

THE NEXT STEP VIDEO SERIES
By Team Wall Street

The advanced version of the Wall Street Workshop™. Full of power-packed strategies from Wade Cook, this is not a duplicate of the Wall Street Workshop™, but a very important partner. The methods taught in this seminar will supercharge the strategies taught in the Wall Street Workshop™ and teach you even more ways to make more money!

In The Next Step, you'll learn how to find the stocks to fit the formulas through technical analysis, fundamentals, home trading tools, and more.

HIGH OCTANE OPTIONS VIDEO SET
By Steve Wirrick

Gain a basic understanding of what options are and how you can profit from them. These videos show you how you can participate in the stock market at a fraction of the cost of buying stocks. Learn how to position yourself to capture explosive and lucrative trends. You'll also learn what Steve calls "The Greatest Money Making Secret in the World." Each video in the eight-volume set comes with both a blank workbook and a filled-in version.

BUILD PERPETUAL INCOME (BPI)—A VIDEOCASSETTE

Wade Cook Seminars, Inc. is proud to present Build Perpetual Income, the latest in our ever-expanding series of seminar home study courses. In this video, you will learn powerful real estate cash-flow generating techniques, such as:

- Power negotiating strategies
- Buying and selling mortgages
- Writing contracts
- Finding and buying discount properties
- Avoiding debt

CLASSES OFFERED

COOK UNIVERSITY

People enroll in Cook University for a variety of reasons. Usually they are a little discontented with where they are–their job is not working, their business is not producing the kind of income they want, or they definitely see that they need more income to prepare for a better retirement. That's where Cook University comes in. As you try to live the American Dream, in the life-style you want, we stand by ready to assist you make the dream your reality.

The backbone of the one-year program is the Money Machine concept–as applied to your business, to stock investments, or to real estate. Although there are many, many other forms of investing in real estate, there are really only three that work: the Money Machine method, buying second mortgages, and lease options. Of these three, the Money Machine stands head and shoulders above the rest.

It is difficult to explain Cook University in a few words. It is so unique, innovative and creative that it literally stands alone. But then, what would you expect from Wade Cook? Something common and ordinary? Never! Wade and his staff always go out of their way to provide you with useful, tried-and-true strategies that create real wealth.

We are embarking on an unprecedented voyage and want you to come along. Yes, it takes commitment. Yes, it takes drive. Add to this the help you'll receive by our hand-trained experts and you will enhance your asset base and increase your bottom line.

We want to encourage a lot of people to get in the program right away. You could save thousands of dollars if you don't delay. Call right away! Class sizes are limited so each student gets personal attention.

Perpetual monthly income is waiting. We'll teach you how to achieve it. We'll show you how to make it. We'll watch over you while you're making it happen. Thank you for your consideration. We hope to see you in the program right away.

Cook University is designed to be an integral part of your educational life. We encourage you to call and find out more about this life-changing program. The number is 1-800-872-7411. Ask for an enrollment director and begin your millionaire-training today!

If you want to be wealthy, this is the place to be.

The Wall Street Workshop™
Presented by Wade B. Cook and Team Wall Street

The Wall Street Workshop™ teaches you how to make incredible money in all markets. It teaches you the tried-and-true strategies that have made hundreds of people wealthy.

Youth Wall Street Workshop
Presented by Team Wall Street

Wade Cook has made a personal commitment to empower the youth of today with desire and knowledge to be self sufficient. Now you too can make a personal commitment to your youth by sending them to the Youth Wall Street Workshop and start your own family dynasty in the process!

Our Youth Wall Street Workshop teaches the power and money making potential of the stock market strategies of the Wall Street Workshop™. The pace is geared to the students, with more time devoted to vocabulary, principles and concepts that may be new to them.

Your children and grandchildren can learn these easy to understand strategies and get that "head start" in life!

If you're considering the Wall Street Workshop™ for the first time, take advantage of our free Youth Wall Street Workshop promotion and bring a son, daughter, or grandchild with you (ages 13 to 18, student, living at home).

Help make your children financially secure in the future by giving them the helping hand in life we all wish we had received.

Financial Clinic
Presented by Team Wall Street

People from all over are making money, lots of money, in the stock market using the proven bread and butter strategies taught by Wade Cook. Is trading in the stock market for you?

Please accept our invitation to come hear for yourself about the amazing money-making strategies we teach. Our Financial Clinic is designed to help you understand how you can learn these proven stock market strategies. In three short hours you will be introduced to some of the 11 proven strategies we teach at our Wall Street Workhop. Discover for yourself how they work and how you can use them in your life to get the things you want for you and your family. Come to this introductory event and see what we have to offer. Then make the decision yourself!

THE NEXT STEP WORKSHOP
Presented by Team Wall Street
An advanced Wall Street Workshop™ designed to help those ready to take their trading to the next level and treat it as a business. This seminar is open only to graduates of the Wall Street Workshop™.

HIGH IMPACT TRADING
By Steve Wirrick
Learn and implement the three pillars that form the foundation of every successful trading program with Steve Wirrick's introductory options seminar. This one day event teaches you how to avoid the six common mistakes people make when trading options, and gives you the tools you need to become a successful options trader.

HIGH OCTANE OPTIONS BOOT CAMP
By Steve Wirrick
The High Octane Options Boot Camp can help you solve the age-old problem of deciding when to buy or sell. At the Boot Camp you'll learn simple trading strategies, step by step, to pull it all together. In this intense two and a half days, Steve reveals his carefully guarded secrets for phenomenal trading success.

EXECUTIVE RETREAT
Presented by Wade B. Cook and Team Wall Street
Created especially for the individuals already owning or planning to establish Nevada Corporations, the Executive Retreat is a unique opportunity for corporate executives to participate in workshops geared toward streamlining operations and maximizing efficiency and impact.

WEALTH INSTITUTE
Presented by Wade B. Cook and Team Wall Street
This three day workshop defines the art of asset protection and entity planning. During these three days we will discuss, in depth and detail, the six domestic entities which will protect you from lawsuits, taxes, or other financial losses, and help you retire rich.

REAL ESTATE WORKSHOP
Presented by Wade B. Cook and Team Main Street

The Real Estate Workshop teaches you how to build perpetual income for life, without going to work. Some of the topics include buying and selling paper, finding discounted properties, generating long-term monthly cash flow, and controlling properties wihtout owning them.

REAL ESTATE BOOTCAMP
Presented by Wade B. Cook and Team Main Street

This three to four day Bootcamp is truly a roll-up-your-sleeves-and-do-the-deals event. You will be learning how to locate the bargains, negotiate strategies, and find wholesale properties (pre-foreclosures). You will also visit a title company, look at properties and learn some new and fun selling strategies.

BUSINESS ENTITY SKILLS TRAINING (BEST)
Presented by Wade B. Cook and Team Wall Street

Learn about the six powerful entities you can use to protect your wealth and your family. Learn the secrets of asset protection, eliminate your fear of litigation, and minimize your taxes.

Call 1-800-872-7411 for a current schedule and product information.

ASSORTED RESOURCES

WEALTH INFORMATION NETWORK™ (W.I.N.™)

This subscription Internet service provides you with the latest financial formulas and updated entity structuring strategies. New, timely information is entered Monday through Friday, sometimes four or five times a day. Wade Cook and his Team Wall Street staff write for W.I.N.™, giving you updates on their own current stock plays, companies who announced earnings, companies who announced stock splits, and the latest trends in the market.

W.I.N.™ is also divided into categories according to specific strategies and contains archives of all our trades so you can view our history. If you are just getting started in the stock market, this is a great way to follow people who are experiencing above-average returns. If you are experienced already, it's the way to confirm your feelings and research with others who are generating wealth through the stock market.

IQ Pager™

This is a system that beeps you as events and announcements are made on Wall Street. With IQ Pager™, you'll receive information about events like major stock split announcements, earnings surprises, important mergers and acquisitions, judgments or court decisions involving big companies, important bankruptcy announcements, big winners and losers, and disasters. If you're getting your financial information from the evening news, you're getting it too late. The key to the stock market is timing. Especially when you're trading in options, you need up-to-the-minute (or second) information. You cannot afford to sit at a computer all day looking for news or wait for your broker to call. IQ Pager™ is the ideal partner to the Wealth Information Network™ (W.I.N.™).

Option Explorer Software
By Steve Wirrick

Use the formulas and equations employed by multi-millionaire professional traders and billion dollar investment houses alike. Option Explorer puts the power of Nobel Prize-winning formulas just click away. The Option Explorer CD-ROM is comprised of the following four distinct programs: Profit & Loss Analysis, Pricing Calculator, Volatility Calculator, and Probability Calculator

The Incorporation Handbook
By Wade B. Cook

Incorporation made easy! This handbook tells you who, why, and, most importantly, how to incorporate. Included are samples of the forms you will use when you incorporate, as well as a step-by-step guide from the experts.

Travel Agent Information
By John Childers and Wade Cook

The only sensible solution for the frequent traveler. This kit includes all of the information and training you need to be an outside travel agent for a stable company. There are no hassles, no requirements, no forms or restrictions, just all the benefits of traveling for substantially less every time. Call 1-800-453-2513 for more information.

EXPLANATIONS NEWSLETTER

In the wild and crazy stock market game, *EXPLANATIONS* Newsletter will keep you on your toes! Every month you'll receive coaching, instruction and encouragement with engaging articles designed to bring your trading skills to a higher level. Learn new twists on Wade's 11 basic strategies, find out about beneficial research tools, read reviews on the latest investment products and services, and get detailed answers to your trading questions. With *EXPLANATIONS,* you'll learn to be your own best asset in the stock market game and stay on track to a rapidly growing portfolio! Continue your education as an investor and subscribe today!